YOUR BROKEN HEART IS ART

A Collection of Words on Becoming, Loving, Emerging, and Soaring

By Sarah L. Harvey

Copyright © 2020 Sarah Harvey

All rights reserved. No part of this publication may be reproduced, distributed, or transmitted in any form or by any means, including photocopying, recording, or other electronic or mechanical methods, without the prior written permission of the publisher, except in the case of brief quotations embodied in critical reviews and certain other non-commercial uses permitted by copyright law.

Although the author and publisher have made every effort to ensure that the information in this book was correct at press time, the author and publisher do not assume and hereby disclaim any liability to any party for any loss, damage, or disruption caused by errors or omissions, whether such errors or omissions result from negligence, accident, or any other cause. This book is not intended as a substitute for the medical advice of physicians. The reader should regularly consult a physician in matters relating to his/her health and particularly with respect to any symptoms that may require diagnosis or medical attention.

For the ones
Who never stopped
Being wild.

For my parents, dearest friends, and love
Who inspire and support me
Every damn day
With their warm, caring hearts.

Acknowledgements

A thousand thank yous to Elephant Journal for their continued encouragement and for publishing so many of these pieces. Thank you to the Urban Howl. Thank you to Michelle Catanach for editing this book so beautifully. Thank you to Katie Hart, for being the best writer friend ever. Thank you to my wonderful readers. May we rise together.

Contents

Introduction — 1

PART 1: BECOMING — 5

1. A Badass Truth-Soaked Manifesto To Help Us Live Like We Really Mean It — 7
2. An Empath's Manifesto: I Am Meant To Feel It All — 12
3. Back To The Ocean Inside — 20
4. Confessions Of A Recovering People-Pleaser: I Am Afraid Of My Voice — 21
5. Fuck Happiness, I'll Take Freedom Instead — 25
6. Fuck Perfect. I'll Just Be Me — 29
7. Her Journey. My Journey — 34
8. I Am Not Broken, As It Turns Out — 38
9. No, I Am Not Broken. I Am Becoming — 45
10. I Am Not Who I Used To Be, But I Am Scared Shitless To Be Who I Really Am — 51
11. The Subtle & Sexy Confidence Of Turning 30 — 57
12. There Are Times When I Hate Being Highly Sensitive — 63
13. When Self-Love Becomes Real, Raw & Tender Beyond Belief — 68

PART 2: LOVING — 73

14. A Touch Isn't Just A Touch — 75
15. Expect To Be Loved In This Ecstatic Way — 79

16. I Am Ready For A Man Like You	86
17. I Don't Need Anything Fancy—Just You	91
18. I Had To Be Broken So I Could Meet You	95
19. I Love You, But I Have To Let You Go	98
20. I Miss You Today	103
21. I Will Make The Ending Of Our Love Into My Most Brilliant Blooming Yet	108
22. I'm Not Sure I Can Forgive You, But I Can Forgive Myself	113
23. I'm Hungry For You	116
24. Love Brings Up Our Shit—Messy, Complex & Beautiful	118
25. Love Was Always Here: A Moment Of Unforgettable Beauty	123
26. Maybe Love Is Like A Firefly	127
27. Real Love Is An Adventure. Real Love Takes Balls	134
28. Sacred Sex: I Know Him & He Knows Me	139
29. The Art Of Loving Loneliness.	142
30. To My Future Love—When We Finally Meet, Let's Take It Slow	149
31. With You, I Feel Like Fire	155
PART 3: EMERGING	**159**
32. A Sweet Love Letter For Your Tired & Broken Heart	161
33. An Open Letter To Those Who Love Someone Struggling With Ptsd Or Trauma	166
34. For The Free-Spirited Females With Fiercely Sensitive Hearts	172
35. Freedom: Just You, Your Breath & The Universe	175
36. My Heart Said To Be Gentle. So I Listened	178
37. Pain & Difficulty Give You Wings	182
38. Silence Speaks. Listen.	185

39. Sit Courageously In The Fires Of Your Struggle	187
40. This Is For The Tough Days	190
41. Use The Blessing Of Heartbreak To Create A Brilliantly Beautiful Life	194

PART 4: SHE. IS. SOARING — 201

42. And Then She Left	203
43. Because Now She Remembers	207
44. For The Women Who Are Meant For More	212
45. How To Touch Her	218
46. I Am A Woman. I Am The Medicine	223
47. She Came Back To Life	227
48. She Chose Her Own Heart	230
49. She Dives Deep To Be Reborn	236
50. She Is Not	240
51. She Is Your Challenge—If You're Up For It	244
52. She Said Yes	249
53. The Aquarius Woman	253
54. There's Nothing Like The Magic Of A Woman	257

Introduction

A poem is not just a fumbling of words splattered onto the page: it's a way home to ourselves.

This is what I have learned, in the most trying times of my life.

Creativity is like a breath when you can't remember how to breathe: life-saving, necessary, and magical, as it fills our lungs with a freshness that tastes of honey and citrus, wide open fields, and really great sex.

It can give us beauty, when all we see is pain.

It can tinge the past with newfound power as we crumple it up and write a brand spankin' new story.

It can be wildfire and soothing water at the same time—burning away toxic shit while revealing oceans of strength through salty tears.

That's where these words came from: the depths, the joy, the discovery, the shock and rawness of it all.

Creativity was there beside me the whole time, egging me on. Telling me to go deeper, sweeter, higher, lower.
To explore it all.

I realized I could make anything into art, even panic and pain.

No part of me had to be left out or cast aside. No part was too dark, too passionate, too much, too soft.

I realized that my broken heart is art.

So is yours.

Anything can be art. It doesn't have to be pretty or shiny.

Loneliness, loss, grief, joy, rage, courage, confusion, disappointment, thirst for change, peace, frustration—it can all be art.

It can all be fuel for transformation, nourishment, and blossoming.

Make something today, without giving a damn if it is 'good'.

That is my biggest hope.

Join me.

This is my collection of becoming, loving, emerging, and soaring.

Let your hair down.
Write some poems to put under your fingernails.

Get messy.

Lick the moon.

Sweat, cry, be honest with yourself.

Find creativity as a path to liberation. To healing. To the breathtaking resonance of your own voice.

To the spark inside you that *never died*.

And don't ever forget:

Your Broken Heart is Art.

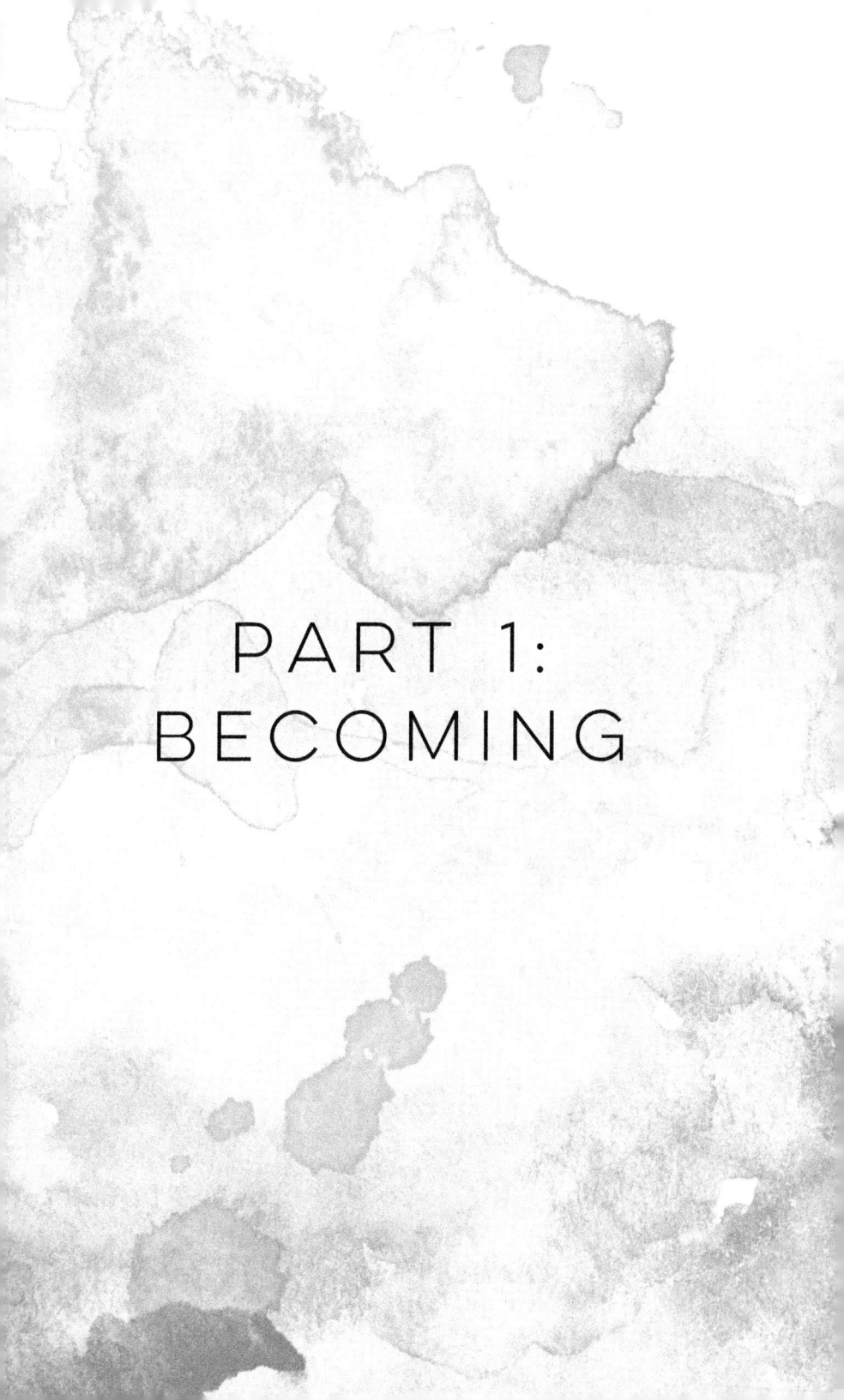

PART 1: BECOMING

1.
A Badass Truth-Soaked Manifesto to Help Us Live Like We Really Mean It

We all have those moments where life slaps us in the face, knocks the wind out of us, and wakes us the hell up.

We realize we have to change the way we're living—our relationship with life itself turned sour, toxic; we cannot wait a second longer to heal the frayed edges, turn the tattered yellowed pages, and write a crisp, brand new story.

This is my manifesto. This is my break-up with the past. This is my badass, truth-soaked fresh start, my new page, scribbled in a furious cloud of hope and wistful freedom.

I wrote it with tears and sweat and deep smiles, and I hope it just might resonate with the delicious longings in your heart too. Let us rise up together. Let us step into the beautiful lives we truly deserve. Let us kiss the sky and live vividly, boldly, soulfully. Let us live like we really fucking mean it.

I hereby undeclare the war on myself.

I am done picking fights with my heart, raging epic battles with my soul, and telling my intuition to shut up.

I am done denying who I really am.

I'm done muting my roarin' goddess voice down to a hoarse, pathetic whisper. I'm done erasing my vibrant, neon colors and appearing to the world in scrambled frames of black and white. I'm done pretending I have no power, that I'm a helpless victim of circumstance, that I don't know how to rise like the bravest phoenix.

That crap ain't gonna fly anymore.

'Cause I can move mountains and I know it. Why deny it for a moment longer?

It's time to live in juicy technicolor, with moonbeams woven in my hair, truth dripping from my mouth like mango juice, and love oozing from my heart like a river of rubies that follows me everywhere—a raw silk scarf, a constant companion.

Gone are the days where it feels okay to recklessly abandon myself. Finished are the moments where it seems brilliant to destroy myself. Done are the years where I pleased everyone but myself.

I hereby undeclare the war on my own heart.

At ease, my heart, at ease!

I need to breathe. Deeply. Softly. I need to remember the exquisiteness of my fiercely feathered soul.

'Cause I am done thinking people are doing me an epic favor when they like me. I am done apologizing for every step I take, every word I utter, every breath I take.

I am done leaning on lame piles of flimsy excuses and selling myself so terribly short.

I hereby declare a confetti-lace peace treaty to celebrate my awesomeness, my one-of-a-kind messy beauty, my huge imperfect heart, my thirsty mermaid soul.

I declare love.

I declare freedom, truth, and blossoming beauty so big it could swallow the cobalt blue sky.

I declare to never, ever forget the gem-like luster of my worth.

I declare adventures that taste muddy and raw, like just-melted snow in the Spring.

From here on out, I will live like I mean it. I will live from the quivering depths of my soul.

I will reach out and taste each day on my tongue, picking moments like ripe cherries, coming alive with the honeyed sunrise, saying yes to even the faintest whispers of truth—the sweet breezes of spirit that keep me alive.

I will slow down and smell the roses and honeysuckle and crisp, musky evergreens.

I will stand tall and say the shit I need to say.

I will move through tears and tough times with the gentlest grace.

I will speak to myself kindly.

I will love fiercely.

I hereby grant myself the most awesome life possible.

I grant dancing under moonlight and sprinting through grassy mountain meadows and writing poems with stars as pens and kissing the cool night air as it tickles my skin, covering me in a blanket of goosebumps.

I will take each day like a lover, suck truth from moments with a straw of a stardust, and make out passionately with the passing seconds as they stream through my fingertips, like sand.

I will color in each morning like a blank canvas with the raw crayon drippings of my soul.

Gone are the times where it felt okay not to honor myself. Finished is the mistaken thought that self-confidence is arrogance. Done are the days where it made sense to destroy myself.

I'm in the driver's seat now—and I'm headed to love. I'm barreling towards truth. I'm running towards myself. I'm rushing towards soul.

There are no excuses left, there is no obstacle in my way, there is no one left to blame.

Loving myself is the only option. Going forward is the only path to take.

Hello world, meet my flames

Meet my gushing wildness

Meet my goddamn confidence

Meet the ballsy twinkle in my eyes

Meet the tornado of empowered truth funneling like lightning bolts through my fingertips as I run free through fields of frost-tipped forsythia, gathering inspiration by the overflowing handful.

Goodbye numb shadows. Goodbye torturous half-life. Goodbye shame.

It's time to say goodbye to bullshit and hello to love.

I hereby undeclare the war on myself.

I am done fighting.

Because it's time to fly. It's time to believe.

My wings are aching, the sky shouts my name.

The past closes, a dusty chapter behind me.

I shake and cry but it's time.

It's time to say goodbye to bullshit.

And say hello

To love.

I hereby undeclare the war on the myself.

2.
An Empath's Manifesto: I Am Meant to Feel It All

Well, I won't beat around the bush—today sucked.

We all have those days when we feel like we don't belong. Today was like that for me.

It was the sort of day that exists in a thousand shades of uncertainty and self-doubt.

I wondered if I looked as awkward on the outside as I felt on the inside. I wondered how the heck everyone else looked so put-together and shiny—meanwhile, I feel like I'm drowning.

But we all have days like this. Especially us sensitive ones.

Sadness explodes like fireworks that give way to tears and a distinct tightness in my shoulders, a trembling in my chin. Cue the self-criticism parade to begin its epic, colorful stroll down the sidewalk, for this is where I get frustrated with myself:

Why do I have to feel this much?

What is wrong with me?

Why can't I be like them?

Yes, them—*precious them*—the ones who seem to mosey through life without a care. The ones who don't feel things reverberating through every bone of their bodies. The ones who laugh loudly over a bunch of beers and craft clever jokes. The ones who are great at small talk and not getting lost in the thick, dewy webs of their thoughts.

I've spent years trying to be that person.

Surprise—I'm not. I never will be.

I'm glad.

Because when I open my heart like a journal and read her ink-stained pages, this is what I know:

I am made to feel it all.

I am constructed of a raw, wild heart that is gigantic and barely fits in my body. She splatters paint in a million shades of aquamarine and citrus orange and feelings. Oh, there are *so many* feelings.

I am assembled of stardust, raw split-open emotion, and unfinished, messy lines of poetry.

I am made to dive deep and be real.

I am made to taste the pain and love of the world, to know the joyous uproars of the universe.

I am made to shake with courageous vulnerability, throbbing like a strange sea creature in my chest.

I am made to cry in gasping awe at sweeping violins in beautiful songs and be drawn into my imagination over and over and over again with a thread made of moonbeams and all the shit I turned into art.

I am not crazy. I am not too much.

I am alive.

Yes.

I am alive with every color of emotion that enters into me—it is a multifaceted, dynamic existence. And there is never a dull moment.

I love that.

I have spent enough days, weeks, and years hating all of this—and trying to be someone else. It feels good to love it now; to *really* embrace and honor my sensitive, tender soul. Yes, it's time.

So, I sit at my desk after a tough day at work and exhale into the rhythm of these words. As my fingers slap the keys, I go on a thousand adventures within.

I don't even have to leave my home to have glorious travels.

There are rich worlds inside of us all—lush, floral landscapes and terrifying, dark forests. There are lively meadows, sapphire beaches, cracked deserts, and icy mountaintops where I can sit out and look at it all; where it's quiet and the view is so breathtaking that it reverberates through me completely.

I am made to feel it all.

So I own it. I own it deeper, wider, wilder than ever before. I stamp down on the earth and exhale with resounding ferocity, and I bellow from the depths of my belly—softly, powerfully, tenderly.

And then I whisper…

Because I know who I am.

There is a tornado inside me. There are tsunamis. There are slow wading pools.

I am made of ocean salt. I am woven of tears. I am made to feel heartbreak and the glorious balm of laughter rip through my body.

I am made to feel it all.

And sometimes, this makes life a bit…tough. I can seem odd or disconnected. Or awkward. But I *am* connected, because well, I feel things so intensely. I feel other people's pain throb through my body. I feel subtle passive-aggressive remarks stab right into my stomach. I feel love spill into my veins like rubies.

I hear the hidden meaning behind words, the truth behind the lies, and the dreams inside us—the ones gasping for air—that we almost let die.

I taste smeared mango-strawberry sunsets with my whole being.

I notice a lot—more than I'd like to sometimes. Crowds are hard and exhausting. Loud noises feel awful to me.

I am an empath, a sensitive soul—and so very human.

I have spent a lot of my life walking around like I don't belong; like I'm too weird, like I have a tail and gills, while everyone else has legs.

But I belong. I have a right to be here—to exist and to live my life with wonder.

And so do you, dear sensitive one.

We belong.

We were made to feel it all.

We dive into the mysterious depths that some cannot even fathom. We face our shit. We paint. We dance. We write. We sing.

We harness emotion from the shaking heights and gorgeous, glittering depths within us.

We hold space for others' healing.

Yes, it can be overwhelming. Destabilizing. Lonely. Tiring. But I would never choose anything else. Would you? I bet you wouldn't.

Because you are brave.

And I know we may be told countless times to become something else—a numb, compliant creature. But we must hold true to who we are.

So no, I will never bend to the world wishing I would just "toughen up." I am a different kind of tough, for I feel everything. And yes, I believe in boundaries, but I don't believe in armor.

I have said it often, and I'll keep saying it every day of my life:

I am not too sensitive.

I am not too soft.

I do not feel too much.

I do not care too deeply.

This is who I am.

And I own the watery depths of my heart completely. Every. Last. Ounce.

Say it with me!

Roar it from the mountaintops of your heart and the great salt lakes of your soul.

I am not too sensitive.

I am not too soft.

I do not feel too much.

I do not care too deeply.

This is who I am.

And I own the depths of my big, watery heart. Every. Last. Ounce.

When we honor ourselves like this, we begin to protect and care for our sensitivity. And this is what we have thirsted for all of our lives: to really embody who we are.

You're *so* beautiful, sensitive one—I feel the beat of your glorious, goddamn powerful, gentle heart.

I feel the way you've been told to cover up your gifts with the glossy fakeness life seems to demand.

Let's call bullshit.

The world does not need us to become hardened.

More than ever, it needs our care, our realness, our joy, our tenderness, and the gritty pearls of our honesty. It needs our ability to feel deeply.

Yes.

Oh, I imagine sweet tears running down our cheeks and pooling into a grand river that becomes an elixir that is messy and colorful and so very healing.

We will never stop being sensitive. Thank goodness!

We will never stop diving deep, growing, rising, transforming, and basking in ecstatic goosebumps painted all over our bodies by the swelling crescendo of the fragrant spring breeze.

We will never stop telling our truths and singing our stories.

We will never stop delighting in our vivid, wide-open hearts

And letting

Life

In.

Don't ever forget, my dear sensitive friend —

We were made to feel it all.

3.
Back to the Ocean Inside

The sun warms my face.
Quiet reaches out and holds me.
I stop trying
So
Hard
To be everyone and everything and
I am put back together
In the immense tenderness
I feel
When *I just am.*
There are no words.
Sensations flood me.
Back, to the ocean inside.
To the thing within us that is ancient
And knows.
Trust this, I am learning.
As waves crash upon soft sandy shores
And say
Welcome home.
I say nothing
And feel it all.
I lick salty waters
As the sun warms my face
Golden & pure.

4.
Confessions of a Recovering People-Pleaser: I Am Afraid of My Voice

I have spent my life catering to the carefree whims of others, trying so hard to say all the "right" things and do all the "right" things and be all the "right" things.

I have lived solely to please everyone, anyone, someone.

And let me tell you—it has been exhausting.

I've become a world-renowned expert at suppressing my needs and smiling pretty when I'm actually sad.

This does not agree with my juicy soul, *at all*.

She has suffered tremendously, slowly suffocating in poisonous clouds of deafening silence.

She grieves, now, for all the times I suppressed myself to disturbing degrees.

For the times I cast shadows on my sparkly spirit. For the times I choked out my opinions like pesky weeds. For the times I pushed down my succulent truths, walking silently on shattered eggshells instead.

She cries roaring rivers for all these painful memories and blooms, white roses of pure forgiveness from the mud of tough, yet crystal clear realizations.

Yes, it's time to move forward.

I am ready to throw away all the forced smiles and false pretenses so I can run wild through wide-open wheat fields and catch clusters of stars with my bare hands.

I am ready to live.

I am ready to hear *me*—my voice, my spirit, my soul, my needs.

I am ready.

As my voice explores the boundless edges of her newfound freedom, she is still shy, shaky and unsure.

She trembles sweetly in her pink polka-dotted rain boots, showing a feeble, yet toothy little smile under her windswept bangs.

She guides me to my heart, showing me something I'd rather not see:

I am so afraid of her.

I am afraid of my own voice.

I am afraid of her roaring fierceness.

I am afraid of her velvety soft gentleness.

I am afraid of her raw, unedited realness.

I am afraid of her intolerance to bullshit.

I am afraid of her wispy tendrils of whimsy.

But, it all comes down to this:

I am afraid to speak my truth.

Because who gives a fuck what I have to say?

My soul stops me, says that she gives *at least three thousand fucks* what I have to say, and urges me onward.

She tells me to take the honesty up a notch or two or ten thousand.

She tells me to bare fluttering butterfly-like vulnerability for all to see.

So I do.

So here it is:

I am afraid to speak because I don't want people to reject me.

But, you know what?

All my worst fears have come true.

I started to speak my soul's truth and voice my opinions and people did reject me. Criticize me. Scold me.

I lost friends.

What a blessing!

Because I see that these are not the people I want in my life, anyway.

I see that I can survive rejection and criticism, no matter how they sting my sensitive skin.

I see that I can hold my own—that I always could.

I see that I can live with not being loved by every single person in the world.

I see the most important thing of all—*that I can say what I need to say.*

Because my voice, even shaky, is a beautiful force to be reckoned with.

So is yours.

Let's honor them, all the way to the stars past Pluto and back.

Let's scream and howl to the moon and grassy ground and foamy turquoise seas.

Let's shout for all those times we didn't shout.

Let's roar like lionesses and tigresses and bears, oh my!

Let's roar world-wide and wildly.

And keep on fucking roaring.

As loudly and fiercely as we can.

5.
Fuck Happiness, I'll Take Freedom Instead

I've wasted my life trying to be happy.

I've relentlessly stalked and chased after Mr. Super-Sexy, Ever-Elusive Happiness, but I'm done.

I've come to see something:

He's not worth it.

I deserve more. You deserve more.

We all deserve so much more.

I don't want him.

So, I'm telling him to stop with his seductive stares because he's actually an empty-headed jerk. He's so flirty, wrapped up in pretty gold wrapper, and it's nice, it really is nice…

But, pretty gold paper isn't gonna do it for me. It's great and shiny and sparkly but it's not what I'm going to live for.

I want more.

I crave more.

I'm thirsty, and…

I don't just want to smile lamely, laughing and giggling, bubbling with saccharine sweetness.

I don't want to be content or comfortable.

I don't want to pretend I'm okay when I'm simmering inside with anger and so, so, so close to screaming out loud into the forest floor.

I don't want to go to your Friday night parties, smiling and nodding politely while nibbling on stupidly fancy appetizers, indulging in your superficial small talk.

No, that's not my goal.

I want freedom. I want depth. I want to live as intensely and authentically as I can.

Happiness won't cut it for me.

I want the whirling gusts of wind to whip around my hair, tasting my cheap cherry-lemon shampoo in my mouth as I run wild through sea-like fields of tall, blonde grass.

I want to feel the warm sun embrace me, growing hotter and hotter until I pour its sweaty kisses from my forehead.

I want to lay alone in the dirt, feeling the earth beneath me, leaves in my hair, crunchy pieces of musky ground covering my hands, getting under my nails.

I want to dance under the winking, twinkling stars, my body moving at dangerous speeds.

I want to drive fast as a falcon, blasting Lana del Rey and screaming to Dark Paradise.

I want to shriek, sob, and shout when I'm angry, sad, jealous, vulnerable, in pain.

I want to live fiercely, wildly, passionately and fucking freely as possible.

I want to feverishly question everything, never satisfying my desperate thirst for knowledge.

I want to be unapologetically me, cursing real filthy sometimes, waxing real romantic sometimes, but never, ever editing myself to fucking please you.

I want to listen to my feminine wisdom, my intuition, my gut: never taking lightly my opinions, needs or desires.

Happiness is not enough.

I want to smile and I want to taste that joy but it won't define me. Or drive me.

It's not enough.

I want freedom.

I want to feel everything. I want the pain, the joy, the disappointment, the jealousy, the hatred, the euphoria, the sadness, the grief and everything in between.

I want it all.

Oh, sweet freedom, link your arm in mine and let's frolic forever under magical moonlight in mysterious open fields.

Let's not settle for happiness.

It's not enough.

Happiness doesn't make my soul soar, my spirit ignite, my insides buzz with electricity.

I will scream and live and die for freedom.

I will never settle for happiness.

I want and need and desire and thirst for—

Freedom.

Feel that delicious word on your tongue and taste it.

It soars.

Now, I soar—

Into the fiercest, fastest winds, feeling more alive than ever.

6.
Fuck Perfect. I'll Just Be Me

"Why is it so damn hard to be myself?" I muttered one morning over the sound of crashing anxious thoughts and racing hummingbird heartbeats.

I woke up that day wanting to sob.

I opened my eyes and stumbled into a poisonous pool of self-hatred.

I whisked together a beautiful blueberry pancake breakfast and tore myself down, down, down.

Thud.

Hello, worthlessness.

From this dark, self-created pit of despair, I could see my self-confidence scamper off into the cloudy morning sky while my self-respect shrugged and ran off, too.

I felt so small.

Panic was ready to pounce.

And, well, panic attacked me, no holds barred. It came on with such cruel ferociousness that I swear I was in a sweaty palmed, glossy-eyed hell from 8:45 a.m. to 10:28 a.m.

I stood idly by as my fluttering, beast-like fears beat the shit out of me.

I struggled for air as salty, worried waters filled my lungs and tried to drown me.

Gasping, I choked violently on seaweed and self-doubt.

And, then, suddenly, as it always does, panic left the building.

I exhaled.

I sat there, panting, reeling from the grand painfulness of it all.

As the waves in my heart become a smooth, sparkling sea, I felt something profound: this overwhelming desire to fuck trying to be perfect. To fuck pretending. And to finally just be me.

Yes, to just be me.

Those thoughts felt good. Really good. I could feel a deep buzzing in my belly along with the sweet promise of feisty little embers that would soon make a roaring fire in my soul.

I felt downright giddy and excited.

Because I've never been me.

I've always papier-mâchéd shiny sequins onto my spirit that other people thought would look good on me.

I've always sugar-coated my words and shoved my own opinions deep down my throat.

I've always bent over backwards to be liked and admired and accepted.

I can't do it anymore.

Trying to be perfect is perfectly pointless.

Living to please others is not living at all.

So, I'm saying fuck no to perfect and fuck yes to being me.

How?

By not trying so hard, for once.

By standing firm as an Oak tree, rooted in the pure magnificence of my identity.

By letting my sore spirit soar into swirling gusts of wind and spread her wings wider than wide.

By speaking my truths loudly, even when I'm shaking like mad, about to cry.

But most of all…

By listening to myself.

Yes.

I will hear my heart's pleas—anxious or not, panicked or not, sad or not—and spritz her with luscious drops of caramel laced love.

I will hear my soul's screams, sobs and giggles, and honor her supreme, roaring fierceness.

I will look at myself in the mirror and say so tenderly: "What do you need, my dear?"

And, then, I will perk my ears patiently and listen so hard.

Shhh…

Come with me.

Do you hear your precious heart thump, thump, thumping?

She's powerful.

She's beautiful.

What does she sound like?

What does she say?

Sit down, put your hand to your chest, and stay awhile.

Don't look away from you own radiance.

Look right into it.

Be blinded by it.

Do you see who you are?

It's written right on your heart.

You just forgot it was there.

You can be reminded anytime.

Anytime.

So, beautiful soul, say it with me.

Fuck no to perfect.

Fuck yes to being me.

Then say it again, louder.

And again.

Even louder now!

Say it until you run out of breath

From the sheer ferociousness

Of your empowered

Fiery screams.

Fuck no to perfect.

Fuck yes to being me.

7.
Her Journey. My Journey

Her path didn't look like anyone else's.
It seemed stranger, sweeter, darker, subtler, angrier.
She liked quiet, and the world was always so loud.

She liked the nothingness, the glorious emptiness, the way silence pooled in her eardrums, like snow falling in a wide-open field.
She longed for the stillness of a slow Sunday afternoon.

But she thought she needed to be sparkly.
As loud as the roaring billboards around her.

She forgot to see that in the peaceful womb of her quietude—
She *did* sparkle. She glowed.

Heaven kissed her lips
And pine trees bent to give her blessings, as she patted their trunks gently
And bowed down to their thick, luscious roots.
Her greatness wasn't tied up neatly in a pink bow
Oh, no—

It was amassed in the trauma, the heartbreak, the rejections, the pain, the irony.
It was messy
Raw

Tender
Terrible
Gorgeous
And so very real.

Her path didn't look how she expected it to.
She quaked with insecurity.
She looked around desperately to see how everyone else was doing it
And tried unsuccessfully, to copy them—
Until the Great Mother herself melted down in a sorbet sunset
Tinged with fire and tingling with truth.
And reminded this woman
What is was to be loved
What it was to belong.

Because she always did—she belonged to nature, to truth, to wings, to poems that haven't been written yet, to the healing of the world, to hope, to resilient moss grown in the cracks of sidewalks, to every woman who howls and wakes up.
But it wasn't until
She felt the Great Mother kiss her cheek
That she wept silently
And knew
It was enough.
Her path was not something to announce loudly.
It was not something that needed to be anything.
It was just for her.

And so, she bit her lip, smiled at the tall, graceful Oak trees, and
began to trust it.
She moved with liquidity, with grace.
She moved like water
And she forged her own damn trail.
She flowed and flowered with abandon now.

Because this—
This, as Great Mother whispers into the cupped shells of her
fingertips—
This is what she was always meant to do.
And it dripped with quiet power.
It dripped with enough love and gentle sincerity to change the
world.
It dripped with the understanding of what it is to hurt, to ache,
to feel forsaken, to taste the bitterness of not fitting in.
This is what made her heart gigantic.
Like fireflies misting over the sky at dawn,
It was a miracle,
She was.

And her path was hers.
It was not expected or worn out or cliché.
It was not something that happened to her.
It was something she co-created.
So she chose to *own it*.
And in owning her path, the succulent solitude, the
serendipitous wisdom—
It began to feel more like

A home
Than a blindingly difficult trek to a so-called perfect destination.

It could be as simple as watching the leaves dance to the ground in Autumn,
Tasting the breeze wrap across her cheeks,
Smelling the citrus-soaked sun at midday
And feeling specks of dirt stuck beneath her fingernails.
It was perfect
Because it was just for her.

In the so-called subtleties, unfurled her power.
It was ancient.
It was great.
It was the key to everything.
She held it close,
Not like a secret
But as something to cherish.
And never
Ever
To tame.

8.
I Am Not Broken, As It Turns Out

There are parts of me that your abuse did not touch.

There are unbroken meadows, pristine peaks, and lush valleys with ferns that hang heavy, soaked with fresh droplets of rain that illuminate in the warmth of the liquid gold sun.

There is renewal.

And yes, there are cracks that exist simultaneously.

There is pain that underlies pain; there is an ache that still throbs every now and then—when my mind wanders, and the tears sting, and I remember what it was like to be close to you.

The closest thing to hell I have ever felt.

But what I need to know right now, is this—

There are places within *me*

So sacred

So pure

So vibrant

No poison words or lies

Manipulations

Or threats

Can live there.

This is my unruined garden.

There are lush roses that lace the air with sweetness.

There are fields rich with lavender that dance in the breeze and perfume my entire body with a light herbaceous scent as they move delicately against me.

Yes.

They are expansive and endless.

They want for nothing.

They were somehow tended to the whole time—

Unknowingly

By me

By hope

By fear

By love

By barely holding on

By all the toxicity that became the most beautiful shit

To fertilize

And make these roses *so damn sweet.*

As I weave through this inner landscape, a deep tenderness flows from secret vines and veins—

It gives way to peace.

The fact that I could feel so peaceful, now

After everything.

The fact that my peace, my spirit, my passion, my thirst for life—

It

Can't

Die.

Even though I felt scraped up, worthless, bloody, dizzy, and confused from all the mind games and cleverly concealed bullshit—

Beauty remains.

Beauty never left.

This is my unruined garden.

You can't have it.

You can't hurt it.

You can't crumple it.

Nothing can.

It is mine.

Forever untarnished

Forever untamed

This is my song, my call, my resiliency.

This is my fire.

It is where my spirit crackles with passion, where my creativity erupts and boils over into lava that leaks onto the page, with purpose so hot I fear I'll melt the computer keys.

There are cracks inside me, yes—I'll be honest about that.

Anyone would feel raw and exhausted after what I've known.

But I am not broken.

And yes, I have to remind myself of this when my lungs singe with panic—when all the heavy, metallic memories and smoke fill my mind with the twisted things you did to me.

But as for me—

I am not broken, after all.

All that you thought was weakness is actually my power.

Nothing can ruin me.

I gush with purpose and fluidity.

I burn with the determination of a falcon diving beside a 50-foot waterfall.

I am unstoppable, as it turns out—

I am the force that keeps going, always—when it's cold and dark, when it's treacherous and uncertain and the light seems just about to be snuffed out.

I didn't let it. And I never will.

I am not broken, as it turns out.

I am regenerative, pure, able to grow back strong, wilder, riper, louder.

I only get better and bolder.

I will always rise again.

I am the day.

I am the light cracking through the mountaintops first thing in the morning.

There is pain, yes—

It lingers, it heals at its own pace—and that's okay.

But I am not broken, and you did not break me.

In this moment, I know the truth.

The truth that resides inside every woman…

I

Am

Glorious.

No matter the traumas that have touched me,

I am still me, still here, still whole, still soft, still wild, and unruly as fuck.

This is what I know.

Resin flows from my wounds; it drips with the songs and screams that become this poetry —

This untapped expression that grows and grows and widens into a net big enough to cast the entire planet.

This is my unruined garden.

My fingers dance in the light as I surface from the depths of the mud — and lilacs rain down in hues of amethyst and white.

This is my voice.

This is my truth.

Your Broken Heart is Art

Nothing can ever

Take

This

From

Me.

Not even you.

9.
No, I Am Not Broken. I Am Becoming

I sit here and reassemble myself

In the quiet moments
When no one is looking.

And something inside rips open, like the searing sea when you can see nothing but water—nothing but the old pain and the whitecaps of waves

There is no land in sight.

At first, I think I am broken
And it hurts like hell.
I think I am dying.

But I close my eyes to greet a different sort of death:

A death that tastes like integration
Like healing
Like the perfume of change—balsamic and wild, like spruce needles pooling on the forest floor.

I drop to my knees
So my masks can slide down my face.

Skin bare. Exposed. Chest raw.

I am here.

It is hard
It is messy
It is glorious.

I am alive with the thunderous crests of swelling feelings
So I dive in.

Deeper!

Into my hungry heart.
The walls in my rib cage collapse
My armor becomes algae
And sea water splashes on my face.

Salt, courage
And becoming.

That's all I ever want to taste.

I am here.

It is not perfect. But it is splendid.

I unpeel old layers.

They disgust me at first
And then I see their ripped beauty, these so-called inner demons.
I see the grit for what it actually is: love, effort, sheer trial and error.

All the ways I tried to survive

In this beautiful, crazy world.

All the different versions of me I tried to be.

It all drops
To the floor now
And gets reabsorbed into the ocean.

As I get goosebumps
And my tears fall like stars
With each gasping breath.

All that is *not me* falls away.
I let it.

I come undone, so I can become who I am meant to be.

Yes—I become.

Oh, and all the layers that froth and moan beneath the surface
All the parts of my Self
I am excited to explore.

Our waters are *deep*
They are vast
They are resilient.

We are worlds unto ourselves.

Yes, every woman is an entire world, a pulsating universe.

And it is our sacred duty

Your Broken Heart is Art

Our most holy adventure

To
Know
Ourselves
To yell
To curse
To whisper
To dance
To feel
To discover
To go deeper

To the ancient ruins inside
That are actually the most precious parts of us—weird, wounded, obscure, scary, "too much," "too sensitive," intense.

Oh, they are the *best* parts of all.

They shine valiantly in our mouths like pearls
As we eat the sun
And tumble into the ocean
With fresh joy spreading through our bodies and lungs.

Hungry inhales
Precious exhales.

This work, this growth
It is humbling
To become over and over again
To fall to our deaths.

And rise.

And kiss the lips of something Divine
Something bigger than us.

It swells like the fog at 5 a.m.

As we dive *deeper!*

Like the mermaids we are.

I am meant for this, as are you.

I will *never* stop growing.

I am in love with transformation

I will *never* stop growing.

It is encoded like a secret scroll deep in my bones
As saltwater pours through my every vein.

Because I do not drown. I do not suffocate.

I am made to wander these underworld spaces
I am meant to walk on the edge of the mysteries
And lick them with the starving tongue of my soul
And let the world pulse like a heart inside of me

Let it flood me with sweetness, with the pain, the ecstasy, the softness, the loss, the beauty
It lights me up
And sets me on delicate fire

So I can burn
With every sweat-bead of awareness
That stings my eyes
And brings an encore of tears

Change. Let it happen!

Change is the chorus. Fear is absent.

I do not fear change.

I re-emerge from the plentiful depths, more whole.

So no. I am not broken.

I am becoming.

Forever.

And
It
Is
Splendid.

10.
I Am Not Who I Used to Be, But I Am Scared Shitless to Be Who I Really Am

I stand breathless, in the awkward, empty in-between—torn between who I used to be, and who I really am.

I'm like a piece of hopeful paper that's no longer blank, but in all its crazed longing for ink, hasn't quite become something else yet.

I'm a sketch that's still living in the echoing ethers of imagination; a painting that exists only in the gentle smoke-like stirrings of a heart unable to find rest; a love that fails to coalesce.

Yes, the giant, gaping chasm that encapsulates me—the past pulls my hands hard, the future invites me with fierce, ballsy excitement, the present confuses me.

And yet, I can't move.

I stand on a jagged cliff, with one foot in the past, one in the future—both frozen with fear, not jumping, not moving, only staying still—as the expansive abyss of the great unknown swirls like charcoal smoke below me.

I'm not who I used to be, but I'm scared shitless to be who I really am.
Where the hell do I go from here?

Because it's true, I can no longer be who I once was. And yet, being who I really am seems like a far-fetched idea, stitched in the sparkling madness of a gossamer fantasy.

I stand in the bullseye of stormy confusion, biting back the tears that refuse to be bitten back anymore.

The tears stream wildly now, well-meaning thoughts of bravery and elegance unable to keep them back.

Who I used to be—the girl I once was—she's gone, nothing more than the faint fumes of a mysterious memory, written in whispers of sadness, of silence, of shrinking.

And yet, I still feel her, deep inside my chest.

She's not dead.
She's a distant part of me.
Fragmented thoughts. Fragmented feelings. Fragmented breathing.

Pieces of raw emotion peel off my skin and fly around the room—an accidental tornado of all that I feel, of all that I've ever felt.

In the darkness, in the incessant chatter of spinning confusion, in the raw mania of truth, all I hear is my wild heartbeat, like distant thunder.

Thump.

Thump.
Thump.

It grows louder and prouder, as I come home to myself.

Should I jump?

Should I take the risk? Should I become who I really am?

Immediately, I feel that familiar stab of fear in my gut—the fear that stops me from breathing. The fear that's plucked the life from me, like a cruel, icy hand popping off a daisy's head.

I'm scared.

The words that seem to mean everything. The sentence that stops me in my tracks. The phrase that tramples on my bravery and silences my roaring courage.

So what!? I say, today. *So fucking what!?*

It's okay to be scared.

So today, I try something new.

I decide that I'm not really stuck.
I get down off that exhausting cliff of duality. Because maybe the question isn't about *jumping or not jumping, being scared or not being scared*.

Maybe it's not so black and white.

Maybe it's about gradually becoming who we are, like the subtle shading of a raspberry soufflé sunset in an oil painting.

Maybe, with every passing day, with every moment, with every breath, we become just a little more ourselves until we are fully submerged in the soulful truth of our identities.

And fuck, maybe it's not even about becoming anything at all.

Maybe it's just about being—breathing.

We forget, but there is more than moving forward into the future; we can also move side to side. We can twirl; we can leap. We can sashay and spin and stretch and rest—and slide right in the present moment.

Maybe jumping isn't required.

Maybe all we need is a breath. A beautiful dream. A luscious moment alone. A morning spent gazing at streaks of orange-tinged sunlight.

Don't be so certain you already know what you need.
Ask yourself. Really ask.

Maybe you need something different, something unfamiliar,

something unexpected.

There's roominess in asking—openness which spawns breath, which spawns life, which spawns strength.

Simply in opening to ourselves and exploring where we are now, we can begin to feel more free, less stuck.

This tiny feather of freedom—it can mean the world to us.

It does to me.

So I sit down.

I stretch and sway, not so focused on how to move forward, where to go, who to be.

I surrender to the sweet scent of lilacs dipped in hope, exciting whiffs of who I already am, of the beautiful things that seem just a little more possible right now.

And I feel the thing that I've never had the courage to believe: I don't need to try so hard.

I don't need to know how.

So, for this moment, I screw knowing. I screw trying.

Fuck 'em both, for just a succulent second.

I breathe, grounding myself in the steady rising and falling of my chest.

I wander.

I wonder.

I explore this precious moment, diving headfirst into the bouquet of dripping, juicy beauty that's available here.

I sigh, seeing for the first time that I already am everything I need to be.

11.
The Subtle & Sexy Confidence of Turning 30

This weird thing has been happening lately where I feel kind of…confident.

What the heck!?

It's the kind of confidence that comes, perhaps, as I greet the cusp of 30.

Maybe in the past, I would have been terrified by this number with its intimidating three-zero, and the thudding sound of my own, unkept promise that I should have started using anti-wrinkle creams two and a half years ago—and yet, I feel at peace.

It is a luxury to get older.

I love it.

I love the ways we learn, the ways we settle into our skin, the shit we face, the shit we try out and never do again and all the beautiful ways that we begin to refine our visions of what a fulfilling life really means. It's simple. It's delightful and no-frills at the same time.

It's taking things less personally, letting annoying things or smart-ass remarks just roll off our shoulders, because sometimes, it's just *not* about us, at all.

It's knowing that I don't really care if deep wrinkles emerge around my eyes. I kinda hope they do—as *walking, breathing evidence* that I have laughed and lived and cried and been *so vividly alive.*

That's what I wish for, more than anything. I hope I have good stories to tell my grandkids, tales of when I messed up, how I rose from the ashes, and how I found balance in it all.

But I no longer wish to be reckless like I once was—to run around aimlessly without a clear path. That becomes easily exhausting, to be honest.

I still love being wild, but in a different way—in a heartfelt and vulnerable way, where I can serve others, be grounded, sassy, and real.

I don't have so much to prove.

I'm not ashamed to admit I'd rather spend a night alone writing, drinking peppermint tea, watering my plants, and falling asleep well before the stroke of midnight beneath my flannel sheets—rather than out drinking whiskey that burns my throat and dancing until dawn because that's what I think I "should" do.

I'd rather be with my kind, steady man instead of chasing a *flash in the pain,* intense-as-all-getup romance. Nah, I move now instead toward something that's long-lasting and sustains me.

Yes. I am different now, as I stare 30 in the sweet, brilliant face.

A page turns, an entire book closes—*boom*—dust ignites in the winter sunlight to form tiny particles of the past. I look at them floating in the air, admiring, and appreciating all the ways they kicked my ass.

But I am silent and still, as the past is gently carried away by the fragments of hope and time and the knowing that *I am ready*.

The journey only ever continues. We can only ever move forward.

I love this feeling of a new page. A fresh, empty book to splash and spill with midnight blue ink and take great pleasure in, as I write the next story.

The past recedes, the present is here. I greet the future with open arms.

There is mystery, there is uncertainty—and yet, this is all the certainty I need.

As I sit

Feel my feet on the floor

Feel these roots I've cultivated

Feel the container of my body, flesh, and bone.

And close my eyes.

Letting every pore

And cell

Take in

Warm beams of citrus sunlight.

It's soft. It's powerful. It's a little awkward, too—but hey, I'll take it.

I am not small anymore. I feel bigger. Fuller.

I am my right size.

Yes. I am different now, after the trauma, after the drama, after all the highs and lows, and all the messy upheavals that just come with the territory when we are finding ourselves.

I am relating to my power in a brand-new way. It's not that I wish to be extra special or have power over others—no thanks, that sounds awful.

But it's about a healthy, enduring relationship with my voice and all the opportunities that come *when we stand a little taller, sit a little more deeply.*

It's all that becomes possible when we remember that we matter—that we can make an impact, speak up, transform, love freaking hard, go for our goals, and achieve downright beautiful things.

I love getting older.

I love all the ways we become more responsible—like paying our bills on time, folding our laundry somewhat neatly, enjoying our work, and *not* running away when the shit hits the fan.

I love how we are no longer blind to the things that truly matter—like quality time with our friends, our families, ourselves.

I love how we come to see that boundaries are a really good thing. Structure can be freeing. Commitment isn't always a drag. Hard work is awesome. Our excuses really do suck.

Old beliefs blow up as we exhale the smoke and see in a new way—with wiser, more patient eyes.

And within this, there is such an opportunity for enjoyment, for freedom, for brand-new adventure of a totally different kind.

For us to really own our shit, to not be victims, to be strong and soft and real—more ourselves than ever.

I love getting older.

I think it's exciting.

I know our culture is obsessed with the fleeting sparkle of youth—but there is such depth and beauty in aging—in the stories, the wrinkles, the grey hairs, the truths of our elders and ancestors.

It would be amazing to ask them to grace us with their wisdom.

And to actually listen.

It would be amazing if we looked up close at all we've learned through the years and saw our lessons, cellulite, scars, wrinkles, and so-called mistakes as gems.

I love getting older.

I love the sense that there is not so much to prove.

I love this feeling of confidence that is subtle and sexy—and just right.

12.
There Are Times When I Hate Being Highly Sensitive

I weep and press my pain into the page, as though it were flowers I could dry and look at in a year from now—with equal parts fondness, frustration and warmth. Like a photograph of splattering emotions.

Sensations cascade throughout my entire body.

Tears come freely. As they land, each one becomes a word.

"I wouldn't choose this," I think to myself.

Except I totally would. Life is rich. Emotions are rivers. My heart roars with the wildness of nature. Colors are bright. I love so deeply. I feel so much.

I know there is beauty in this, I know it is a gift. It is the tenderness that sews me back together, it is the place that crashes like stardust, the mysterious place where the poetry comes from—

But it feels like shit, too. Like I have no skin. Like other people's energy ripples through me. Like I can taste what they're feeling, too. Like I know things that make no sense to my mind, but my soul understands it, somehow—in a language that is beyond time, beyond thought, beyond life, beyond death.

And that's when it's *really hard.*

Hard to manage. Hard to breathe. Hard to sit still without dropping into what feels like a black hole. It's like I'm on the precipice of something that I doubt anyone would understand.

It's like I am an island, all by myself.

Goosebumps emerge, and I feel the universe hot in my throat. There is so much love and so much beauty and so much hurt, but I don't know if I can hold it all.

And in wiser moments, I remember that I don't need to hold it.

I can let it pour and drip through me.

But sometimes, it feels like the world rips me in two, just from walking out the door. In the hateful ways that people act, the stinging things they say, the way society stomps on women, the way people suffer, the way children go hungry.

I feel it. I can't pretend that it's ever been any other way.

I've tried numbness—and it's a false banner made of cheap plastic, for feelings also seep over the edges. They always plunge into my life somehow.

There is an intensity in this —

I am so soft.

I feel so much.

I am vulnerable.

I am gentle.

I am sensitive.

And I am so goddamn tired of hearing that this is a weakness. That I should 'toughen up.'

Being sensitive is actually my great act of rebellion — because *wouldn't it* be so easy to just armor up, and create a facade that isn't so real, but seems sparkly?

And all of this feels at the forefront now, for some reason — maybe it's the plumpness of the full moon, or that I am steadily growing into fullness of myself.

Because I don't want to armor up anymore. I don't want to pretend to be anything other than who I am.

And so I don't keep it at bay…

Feelings comes like waves, I taste saltwater and swallow bits of the ocean in my tears.

I mermaid around in the darkness, the sweet aquamarine waters that feel like home to me.

I am different. Strange, maybe. I feel what people say is "too much."

But as I breathe here, my heartbeat slows.

Because in truth, I am made for these depths—where feelings reign free, where anger lives, where shame resides, where hope transmutes into God, where beauty shines most brightly.

Yes.

I am made for these depths.

It hurts, and it feels isolating sometimes. But this sensitivity—it's not just an inconsequential part of me—it's such an important part of who I am.

In writing this, a most unexpected strength flows into me.

Because there is water, but there is a secret kind of fire, too. Not fire to prove, to overpower anyone, or even, myself.

It's the sun-like radiant fire in owning the beauty in owning my sensitivity after all these years.

It's remembering all the times that I bought into the bitter lies that I am "too sensitive" for this world; that I should feel less; that I need to harden; that I am the problem; that my sensitivity means I have to take other people's shit; that softness means I'm powerless.

And it's letting them go...

Because in truth, softness is what makes me so powerful. *I source my strength from the gushing water of my feelings.*

I love to care for others. To give my heart, whenever I can.

And there is nothing wrong with that.

Now, those old fears and beliefs part like sticky seaweed and the oceanic depths illuminate their own way.

Sweetness prevails, like music.

And it's this. It's this moment that I hold as it glows—and I cry even more, because I am starting to understand.

It's this.

It's all that happens when we finally begin to wholeheartedly embrace our gifts.

13.
When Self-Love Becomes Real, Raw & Tender Beyond Belief

The rains have rendered my favorite park into a swamp of sorts. Plump irises sit in stagnant brown water, their purple heads bobbing in the gentle wind.

It's actually quite beautiful. It's still.

It—like so many things—is a portal into the kind of spaces we starve for, but don't even know it.

Depth. Quiet. Reflection. Nurturing beauty in the most unexpected places.

I smile, half-heartedly wondering if there are any ferocious crocodiles lurking in these strange muddy waters dotted with indigo irises.

I smile at the thought of this—yet, don't we often fear the same thing when we look within?

We worry what monsters might be there underneath our skin, snarling and gigantic, ready to devour us—ready to freak us out as our legs gear up, ready to run far and fast.

As luck would have it, our inner terrain is usually not as scary as we make it out to be.

There might be something or several somethings, sure—

The frayed edges of the past. Old pain. New pain. Unrealized dreams. Hope that was misplaced, and only partially regained. Disdain with our bodies. Those 10 pounds we never lost. Sharp bits in our hearts that were once broken, but the edges become softer beneath the warmth of our gentlest embrace.

There might be uncertainty. Loneliness. Grief. Doubt.

Do we look away, as we have done a million times before?

Or do we dip a toe in?

Do we dare to dive in, submerging our arms and legs and faces fully?

Because there is something so nourishing about it all—even the not-so-pretty parts that are hidden inside, tucked carefully into shadows, shoved into big, dusty boxes that are kept on the farthest outskirts of our minds.

There is stillness and depth. Wisdom and knowledge.

As we lean in

And learn to hold these shaky, shivering parts of ourselves with care—

Spaciousness prevails.

Your Broken Heart is Art

A gust of wind opens our chests and airs out the shadows inside: *the parts we thought would never be good enough or healed or whole or valuable at all.*

In the sunlight, we see our wounds anew. We see them as pearls.

Incandescent, formed through stress and friction. The result is breathtaking. Nothing less.

They are lustrous and gleaming and real.

So are we.

Through our courage, self-love takes on a much richer quality. It becomes—not just a lovely idea—but a way of living, of being, of connecting with ourselves, the planet, and others. It becomes real.

This type of self-love is as wide and deep as the ocean, as gritty as the dirt on our feet. It contains not only the sparkly, nice things about us that are easy to like.

But every. Thing.

The messy, shy, vulnerable, uncomfortable, squirmy, messy, slightly broken parts are included too. Even the parts we aren't sure we *can* love or tolerate.

Every. Thing.

Unabated tenderness weaves through the air.

Our muscles relax and stop gripping for the first time in ten years.

Breathing becomes a masterpiece. Exhaling is a way to let go without trying. Our eyes soften.

And it doesn't happen in one fell swoop, but much like the rain — one drop at a time. One grateful, salty tear at a time.

Our existence becomes more real.

Gradually, we no longer fear the swamps or murky waters inside. We don't run or numb. We become braver and more vulnerable. We behold the beauty that blooms in the most unexpected places.

As we practice and sometimes stumble, our hearts grow. They become gigantic.

We begin to see love everywhere. In ourselves, others...even in the people we used to hate.

"The only reason we don't open our hearts and minds to other people is that they trigger confusion in us that we don't feel brave enough or sane enough to deal with. To the degree that we look clearly and compassionately at ourselves, we feel confident and fearless about looking into someone else's eyes." ~ Pema Chödrön

PART 2: LOVING

14.
A Touch Isn't Just a Touch

A touch isn't just a touch

It's a kiss from my soul, onto your skin. It's the sensation of your soul, whispering to my fingertips

There is no hurry
There is you
And me
And the way we breathe together in golden alchemy
Timelessness expands out
We bloom for ourselves
For each other
Ruby red hibiscus flowers in the sweet heat of summer
The sky rains petals and drips a sunset of magenta passion.

In moments like this, the world does not exist
All the frantic doing and spinning wheels of busy fade away
There is only the music we make together.
The shouts of raw ecstasy we can't help cry out
The humming hymnals of our hearts
The symphony of fireflies blinking in harmony
The naked prayers we make with our bodies.

And oh, the way your tongue darts delightfully into my mouth.

Your Broken Heart is Art

I dare you to go deeper
Feel *more*
Be *more* naked
Be *more* vulnerable
Expose every part of who you are
And I'll do the same—

Dive in to experience the mystery I am.
Taste my sweet waters
Land on my shores and swim in the currents of my dark, hidden rivers.
Our kisses are keys
Our secrets spill out
The mystery only grows deeper.
As we shine more light on ourselves
On every fractured, whole, beautiful and shaky part

With every breath, every word, every kiss
For love making
Is about making *more love*
More art. More richness. More vividness. More heart. More truth. More bravery, poetry, prayer, and joy.

It is the spark of inspiration that shoots into us like lightning
It is when the masks drops, the veils fade
Nakedness permeates
Like smoke
That rises to the heavens
Alongside the tango beats of our hearts

Passion…
More.
Yes.
Thank you. I love you.

Satisfaction comes at a thousand clips a minute
Tears too
When we take our time
To
Slow down
And feel everything.
Everything fucking thing.
Every fleeting sensation and rising, rippling pleasure and fear and joy and longing

When we wake up to remembering that *sex is not sex*
It is sacred
It is wildness and perfection
It is beauty
It is the way my soul sings
With your soul
And what a song it is!

I get lost in the way it echoes across the mountainside
The way it soars with the falcons
Those melodious wingbeats make us purr and moan in sheer reverence
Of each other.

Your Broken Heart is Art

A touch isn't just a touch
It's the way my soul sings with your soul.
It constantly crescendos and changes
It is the most beautiful thing I've ever heard.

I could listen to it forever.

15.
Expect to Be Loved In This Ecstatic Way

I know it's easy to forget—to buy into the shiny emptiness of what society says we should be…

And feel out of sorts, out of place, unattractive, too much and not enough at the same time

But—

You're breathtaking, my dear woman. It is written in how deeply you feel and how brightly you burn when you remember who you are.

Because you are the earth, lush and wild. You are the expanded lap of the universe.

Why do you make yourself small and bite-sized for him?

Why do you twist, and turn, shave yourself down, and pray that he'll notice?

Why do you try and try to earn his love?

Don't.

You are the explosion of a nebula and the nectar kiss of an ancient sex goddess.

You are the treasure, the truth, the freshness, the medicine.

You are the depth, the roaring, the promise of springtime in a single bud.

You are the messiness, the complete and utter soul-dripping perfection.

Stop wallowing in the arms of a half-assed love that's long wilted.

Instead—

Be

Queen

Dab roses on your wrists, and scent your hair with frankincense and cinnamon.

Re-sanctify.

Re-center.

And be ready for the man who laps up your complexities like they're the marbled tips of the Milky Way.

Be ready for the man who loves your fire and fans your wildness with his hot breath as he kisses you all over.

Be ready for the man who isn't blinded by your light, but honored, humbled, and inspired that a woman could be brave enough to burn so brightly.

Be ready for the man who isn't scared of your fierceness, who respects that you have claws and know how to use them

That you know *what you like*

And don't like.

What you need

And don't need.

Be ready for the man who adores the tender aches etched in the delicate pages of your glorious heart, the chapters and shadows that you once disowned because you thought they were ugly…

Oh, honey—

He'll love those too.

He'll hold 'em close and tuck his fingers into your tender corners with a touch that tastes of cherries and whispers to the deepest places within you.

Because he is able to surrender his armor to the jeweled palace of your unbroken femininity.

Be ready for the man who is exhilarated to see you exalted and *never, ever* succumbing to a life of stagnation or slow decay

But constant radiance, wonder, soul and the catapulted confidence of a Priestess shooting out of the dirt in springtime.

Be ready for the man who does not tremble when you cry and feel deeply.

Oh no, he'll hold space for you—

Lapping up your passionate expressiveness like the grass when it rains, elated and thirsty to taste the honeyed drops like dew with every word you speak.

He'll see you

All of you

The whole you

For the incredible blessing you are.

He won't need you to be small. He'll just need you to be yourself—

Be ready for him—

The man who isn't blinded by your light

But encouraged by it, moved by it…

The ancient energy

That erupts like lightning

It bubbles and shimmies like an earthquake

A sight so exquisite it punctures down to the bone

And brings him to his knees in the sweetest way

Because you're anything but small.

You are the grass, the hope, the roots, the sun, the healing, the death that begins a new life.

You are a woman. You are the medicine.

So stand up—

There is no need to crawl and beg for love

To bend and twist and long for approval from a man who can't see you, who can't show up for you, even on his best day.

The eyes of his heart are closed, sewn shut

And you can't open 'em.

Stop trying.

Stand up…

And don't wait, like those annoying "rules" say we should.

Fuck waiting

Be brilliant

Be peaceful

Be wild

Be magnetic

Be vulnerable

Wave the wand of your heart

And carve your dreams out of the shit

Into beautiful stones of reality

And be ready

Be real

And expect

Yes, expect

The man who will be dazzled

By the way the moon moves in your smile

By the way you squeeze the pain and make it into art

By the way you live and breathe in the deep, blue seas of authenticity

With all the power that's yours naturally

When you stand

In truth

And don't hustle for love.

Be ready for the man

Who can embrace

All of you

But you need to embrace yourself first.

And in that sublime basking on your sacred temple shores

You will then be ready

To embrace the man who can blaze with you, lighting up the sky together in shades of peach and nectarine.

So beautiful

You'll weep

From joy...so much joy!

Expect

To be

Loved

In

This

Ecstatic

Way.

16.
I Am Ready For a Man Like You

I've waited for you forever, but forever is over—I'm done waiting.

I take a more active role now.

I free myself, I heal, I speak, I dance, I live—I pour my heart out and laugh—stepping boldly out of years of silence, suffering, masks, pretending and epic disguises.

I stand naked, without any armor whatsoever—for I know that to find real love, *this is how I have to be.*

Vulnerable.

Just me.

It is enough.

For my heart is juicy and open and ready—she seeps out like a ruby sea, no longer willing to apologize for her passion and thrashing intensity, and no longer able to appease anyone by being a shadow of herself.

No, I must be whole. Holy, in all of me.

I run my fingers down my flesh, for my body is ripe. I feel a succulent springtime dance across my skin, blossoming one bud at a time. The air around me smells like mud and the sweet, sultry scent of lilies—damp, but full of hope, like the forest after it rains.

I am subtly confident, coming into the fiery petals of my not-so-subtle femininity, no longer filled with doubt that my quest for love doesn't deserve a downright epic ending.

I ask for what I want—what I need—without shame. And I ask—I long—for you, my love. I call out to you. Because I know that you are already here, longing also for me.

I could never settle again. And I won't. My soul thirsts, my heart roars—*only for you. Only ever for you.*

Do you hear me?

I hear you. I hear you whispering in the winter winds; I hear your pleas to find a woman like me when I sing in the shower as the sun is rising, hot and red, over the mountain meadows I love to dance and run through and scribble poems in.

I am ready for a man like you. There is no lingering question about that. Readiness is all I taste on my lips now.

Yes. I am ready for a man like you—a man who knows his soul is a map to eternity.

A man who laughs hard and kisses softly.

A man who touches me like I'm a marble masterpiece and shoots me to the moon with pleasure like I've never tasted in my life.

A man who is just as warrior-fierce as he is gentle and kind.

A man who can cut the rope of his fears, dust off his old pain—

and keep going.

A man who knows how to pray. And play. And run free. And thinks maybe they're all three the same thing.

A man who loves with *all of* the passionate power in his heart. Every pulsating ounce.

A man who is not perfect—screw perfect—but strong and kind and brave, and always working on himself.

Yes.

I am ready for a man like you—a man who can weather blue skies and wild, stormy days with a wickedly curious smile spread across his face. A man who knows how to weep.

A man who is moved by nature and beauty, humming songs to blossoming buttercup buds and caressing soft, emerald leaves.

A man who hits rock bottom—and chooses to become softer and wiser from tasting the darkest depths of suffering.

A man who can fuck and make love in the same breath.

A man who craves adventure—sudden journeys into shady mountain evergreens, exposing the molten passion of our quaking souls as we read each other poetry.

A man who can honestly love a dangerous woman like me, as I stand firmly in my passion and purpose, never again wavering from the hot truth that vibrates in my voice.

Hear me, hear me—I won't be quiet. I can't tone it down, but I know you'd never want me to.

I am ready for a man like you—a man who can pick up a drill and a freshly cut flower with ease.

A man who wakes in the morning and tastes the milky red sunrise—savoring it, as he does his coffee, as he does his life.

A man who stands up for himself, for others and for this world.

A man who knows how to get shit done.

A man who knows the delicate art of not-doing.

A man who looks at me with his eyes, but mostly, with his soul piercing through.

I am ready for a man like you—a man who knows who he is.

A man who takes no crap and speaks his mind.

A man who lives in the raw, jagged, oceanic depths of life.

A man who is boldly committed, tied at the knot—to his own truth—and the blossoming jewel of his identity.

A man who licks his lips and tastes mine with a frantic fervor like this breath could be his last.

A man who *never* keeps me guessing where we stand.

A man who takes my hand in public proudly.

A man whose brave heart drips down his chin like the ripest mango, because he knows that vulnerability is the answer to almost everything.

And above all—a man who believes that love is a stunning mystery to jump into with both bare feet.

I won't settle.

It's only been you—only ever you.

With open arms, I invite you to the altar of my soul. Bring pink lilies and your wide-open heart—that's all I'll ever need.

Please take good care of my heart, and I'll care for yours like it's my favorite thing in the world, because it will be.

These words rise up in my throat like smoke as I send out this wish—this prayer. It reaches heaven in swirling echoes that smell like juniper and sage and sandalwood.

The embers burn in my belly, my inner fire sparks to life—I burn. For I know it's true.

I am ready for a man like you.

I know you're ready for a woman like me.

And so it is.

The diamond-studded hope of finding love becomes, not any longer a fantasy, but a very delicious reality.

17.
I Don't Need Anything Fancy–Just You

I've missed you.

How does life get so busy? The days—one after another—pile up like a stack of blurry Polaroids on my desk.

"There isn't enough time," we mutter, citing tiredness as our half-assed excuse.

But that's a lie. And we know it.

There's no time?

Let's make some. And after that, we'll make love.

I want to stop, freeze-frame all the madness—and zoom in.

I want to create something beautiful.

I want to stay up all night tangled in the sheets, our bodies covered in sweat with smiles gracing our glistening faces.

The soundtrack will be laughter and our heavy breaths, the moans we make from the careful caresses we sweep across each other's skin.

The setting will be home. Simple. A candle or two.

I don't need anything else. I don't want to be wined or dined. I just want to play, laugh, and be close to you.

I want time to lose all meaning—as our lips meet, the clock stops. And we are so in the moment that we become braided into each other, into the pulsating fibers of the universe itself.

We will rise, we will fall, with the glowing neon filaments of euphoria. We will gush like water and undulate like the ocean, like a supple belly dancer's stomach.

'Cause I don't need anything fancy. I just need you.

The wildflowers in your hands—they're perfect.

Set them down on the kitchen table as you lift me into your arms and our cells crash into each other.

Let's make a date.

I'd like to spend time getting ready and actually shave my legs. I'd like to wear something slinky that makes me feel sexy and womanly—and dab on lip gloss and my favorite sweet, mysterious perfume.

After many busy weeks, after being everything, after going here and there, doing this and that—*we need this.*

Our love must be nourished. We must be fed in this exact way.

Skin on skin, hearts beating wildly, lips locked together. Our tongues can be paintbrushes that flicker in the starlight as we finally—oh, sweet finally—let our bodies relax and melt into the delicious truth of what we really want.

To be close. To be seen and touched and held and known.

We cannot let this sweetness fall to the wayside just to complete our to-do lists.

So, clear a space. Meet me tonight. Say, 7 p.m.

Let's say we're going to cook dinner—but instead, I'm going to kiss you when you walk in the door.

I won't wait.

I want you, right away. Before anything else.

We need this. This moistening, this addition of fresh, juicy life back into our love—back into our bones, our spirits, our lives.

Connection heals, and as our hands join, our bodies sing out and rejoice.

Our chests may still feel weary and armored, but slowly, we breathe together and let it *all* peel away as our hearts bloom to take another shape. And tenderness—oh, tenderness we embody so beautifully.

Everything else fades away. And it's not that we leave anything behind, we simply enter into a parallel universe of just you and me.

You twirl me around and set me lovingly on the bed. I caress your face, then get fierce, becoming the tigress I am.

Touch is joy.

Without nourishment, this love withers. And so do we.

We need this.

So let it all go.

Exhale the week away. Let it blow like smoke into the sky and become a cloud that tucks behind the moon.

Be enraptured in me, in you—in magic. In love.

Yes.

Let the softness of this love carry you through it all.

And sure, we've got this crazy, busy life where we're both trying to pursue our dreams.

But we have each other.

And that's what makes it all beautiful.

So kiss me.

Right now.

18.
I Had to Be Broken So I Could Meet You

It couldn't have happened any other way.
My heart had to be splintered, smashed, just short of shattering completely.
I had to fly low and dive deep.
I had to let myself disintegrate into wounded ashes.
Yes.

I had to be broken so I could meet you.
Because I didn't learn to be myself until I was broken.
The exquisite elixir of vulnerability transformed me.
It opened my eyes and unlocked my heart.

I had to be broken so I could meet you.
Because those jagged shards became beautiful as they opened up new space in my fragile heart.
Space that wasn't there before.
Space I didn't know about.
Space that your heart needed so it could entangle entirely with mine.

I had to be broken so I could meet you.
And you had to be broken, too.
Because when our shattered hearts saw each other for the first time,
They were wise and knew this was real.

Your Broken Heart is Art

We both breathed in, and by the time that inhale transformed into an exhale,
I was yours and you were mine.
A simple transformation, a beautiful alchemical exchange.

I had to be broken so I could meet you.
Of course, I was broken all along.
I just didn't always know it.
Of course, you were broken all along.
You just didn't always know it.
But, it's so lucky we were both destroyed —
Because our fragile hearts slid perfectly together between those sharp shards.
Now fused permanently with glossy golden ribbon,
Our formerly tattered hearts smile and sunbathe in bliss.
Pure bliss.

I had to be broken so I could meet you.
Because being broken made me courageous.
And I needed to be brave enough to show you my flaws,
Which are actually the things you love the most.
And you needed to be brave enough to show me your flaws,
Which are actually the things I love the most.

I had to be broken so I could meet you.
Because brokenness made me real.
You had to be broken so you could meet me.
Because brokenness made you real.
And, what we both wanted

More than anything
Was to be
Real.

19.
I Love You, But I Have to Let You Go

Right now, I want nothing more than to run into your arms, kiss you so hard, and have your soft touch melt every ounce of my pain away.

I want to feel the bristles of your beard rub against my face, as you hold me in a tight, protective embrace.

I want us to laugh and talk for hours and cook dinner together, drinking spicy red wine, chopping up onions and garlic, and making hearty soup for the week ahead—like we always did.

If our fingertips could touch, if our hearts could beat side by side, then maybe everything would feel right in the world again. Maybe my tears would dissolve into smiles, my loneliness would become sweetness, and this goddamn anguish would become a gushing river of love.

How am I supposed to get on without you?

I stand alone, not knowing where to go—unable to figure anything out, unable to think straight. Every minute feels torturously long—strung of a thousand tears, a necklace of grief that swallows me up with sharp teeth.

As the clock slowly clicks on, minute by minute, second by second, as my heart beats—I'm certain that time is frozen, that I'm stuck in an icy palace of heartbreak where the breeze rips through my skin, re-plays our most precious memories and brings me to my knees.

As I pause briefly between the tears, I have this strange wish — I wish that our love was a book, and I could edit the ending, making it happier, less brutal, and less messy.

I wish I could craft the words to be perfectly pleasing to our hearts, and make it an ending where we found a way to compromise without compromising ourselves — where we resolved all of our problems and curled up together, hand in hand, kissing, looking at each other with wild contentment sparkling in our eyes like fire.

Instead, the story of our love is finished. Wrapped up — done. And yet, something still feels painfully unfinished —

I always thought that a break-up immediately snips the thread that connects two hearts, but that's not true.

The thread lingers — it burns, it stings, it pulls, it dances in the wind. Love forever leaves an imprint in our hearts. A residue of some kind. An echo in our bones. Memories racing, at full speed, through our minds.

Maybe our love will always feel unfinished.

And I won't lie, I pray that we will find our way back to each other someday — I pray that maybe this road we're taking is part of the path that will eventually lead us back together.

But high hopes can't sustain me.

For now, our story is finished.

And deep in throes of this loss, in the midst of this swirling sea of grief—I know there is only one thing to do.

I have to keep living.

Start a new story—open a fresh, empty page and grab a pen—cry my eyes out and make something fucking beautiful.

I have to live brilliantly—live artfully—live with my whole, broken heart, with every fiber of my being.

Even though all I want is curl up and hide under a hundred blankets, even though I miss you so much that the ghosts of our sweet memories fill up my bones and weigh me down like lead—

I have to keep living.

I have to keep sketching my story. Chasing my dreams—creating, exploring, learning, laughing. I have to keep prying open my heart and tasting each passing moment on my tongue.

I have to see that there is more to life than falling in love.

I have to live.

Maybe I will embrace loneliness and make art out of it. Maybe I will sprout wings and learn to fly from the ashes of this fierce pain.

Maybe I will listen to my heart's wild calls and travel across the seas and see Bali, live in a sun-soaked town in California, write a book of poems, and finally do all the awesome shit I've always said I wanted to do.

But right now, as the clock clicks slowly—as my heart beats, as my tears fall—all that hangs in the air, like a dense fog, is the fierce wish that we could have made this work. *That it could have lasted a little longer.*

What if?

What if we could have made it work?

As I blink—as more raining tears fall—I breathe slowly, surrounded by a cold swarm of fluttering *what ifs.*

But in a small moment of clarity, goosebumps cover my skin—a subtle softness enters into me, like a distant whisper.

And it's so strange, but I can feel it in my bones—*this was the right thing to do.*

I love you, but I have to let you go.

We have to let each other go.

Our story is over. The final words have been written, the last drops of ink have been spilled, and the story-line is locked in place.

Hard as we tried, we couldn't bridge the gaps between our

differences.

And it hurts, my god, I know it hurts—

Because I love you.

But maybe as we say goodbye to each other, we will be saying hello to something beautiful. Maybe we will be saying hello to our dreams—to the paths our hearts were meant to take.

Maybe we have to see each other free

So we can both finally

Stand up

Look life in the eye

Unfurl our wings

And

Learn

To

Fly.

20.
I Miss You Today

I tried not to think of you today. I tried so hard, but I failed beautifully.

You showed up, as a lone tear streaming down my cheek. You showed up as a shy ghost haunting my thoughts. You showed up, like a piece of prized jewelry, a precious heart-shaped locket that should be sitting proudly on my collarbone, but instead got lost on a busy city sidewalk and now belongs to someone new.

From the moment I woke up this morning, I knew something was missing. My smile, beaming as it was, had holes in it.

There was a stark hollowness in my bones. A tiny rip in the fabric of my heart. Something dark that whispered to me in moments where it got too quiet. Something that ached deeply when the church bells rang at exactly noon.

I went outside to hear them.

With each tender ding, ding, ding—the dancing bells told me the truth.

Something is missing from me—it's you.

Your heart. Your kiss. Your voice.

I can try to pretend I'm not hurting; I can try to pretend I'm strong and brave, but my insides feel like tiny scraps of ripped lace and pretending hurts more than admitting the truth—

I miss you today.

I miss the delicious comfort of curling up beside you, our bodies tangled like pretzels in cozy, satisfied knots. I miss going for long walks, our arms linked together, for what seemed it would be an eternity, our steps matched to the frantic rhythms of our happy heartbeats. I miss talking to you about my day—and hearing about all the tiny, beautiful details of yours. I miss knowing you'd text me when you wake in the morning, with a heart. Always with a heart.

I miss you today.

There are moments where the sudden falling apart of our love feels like too much to bear. The grief comes crashing in waves, ranging from dull, to epic, and full-on unbearable. Right now, a salty wave of unbearable sadness pulses through my body, it barrels rudely through my bones—and I wish you were here. Next to me. Holding my hand. Smiling your crooked little smile. Making stupid jokes.

I don't need you to take away my pain with your presence.

I need to be with this pain.

Alone.

It's the only way.

But my heart still reaches out to you anyway—even though you can't feel it. Or hear it. My fingertips reach out to join yours, but they can't find you through this vast, echoing distance, and my touch can't puncture these icy walls we've built up around us.

For a tiny, tortuous second, I swear I feel your soft kiss in the breeze, I swear I feel you thinking about me, but it's not; it can't be. All that hangs in the cool afternoon air is the unfamiliar scent of a future without you in it.

As the church bells end their song, a painfully beautiful six minutes later, I exhale and swallow sharply, walking back inside slowly to go about my day.

As long as my heart is beating, life must go on.

There are sugar cookies to decorate and family members to drink coffee with and emails to check and tender stories to write. So, I will go about my day. Even though I hurt. Even though I ache. Even though I can't think straight.

As long as my heart is beating, life must go on.

Life must move forward, even if it's moving forward without you.

Because I know deep down, we tried. We tried so hard. We tried too hard. We tried until we were both empty and hollow, exhausted and angry, not a drop of understanding left in our hearts. We tried until we yelled and screamed and couldn't possibly try for a moment more.

We just couldn't close the growing gap between us. We couldn't compromise without compromising ourselves.

And that's okay—our painful parting is a strange relief in its own twisted way.

But, today, it hurts. It hurts like a freshly cut wound. My insides feel like tiny scraps of ripped lace and pretending I'm fine hurts more than admitting the truth—

I miss you today.

So, I make space for missing you. I honor all that you meant to me, because you meant so much. You were a blazing light in my heart, a spark of inspiration to my thirsty world, a warm, tender love who challenged me and changed me, deeply and deliciously.

I honor you.

I can't pretend this pain away, because I don't want to.

I miss you, in this moment, more than I've ever missed anyone.

And that's where I am. It hurts, it throbs, it stings, but it's also okay.

Because this sadness is so goddamn beautiful in its own way.

It's like a dark red rose—ominous, surrounded by wickedly sharp thorns, but full of undeniable hope and unthinkable beauty.

And so is this moment.

Yes. I'm crying. But each tear shimmers with hope, it reeks of beauty, it pulses with the pristine possibility of solitude, of smiles yet to come, adventures yet to take, sweet memories to be made— even though the raw hurt of being without you still rattles through my entire body.

I miss you today, my sweet once-lover.

I miss you a lot.

And that's perfectly okay.

21.
I Will Make the Ending of Our Love Into My Most Brilliant Blooming Yet

It's over—but I don't think our love will end.

It's not exactly written like that, is it?

Our love will run like tears from watercolors and create a new something. Its net will cast wider—deeper into the sea. Back, back, back…to the creations with no legs.

Back to water. To swimming. To feeling. Back eleven centuries when it was all different…simpler.

And, in our breath, spaciousness will leak from our parted lips and our last kiss—the distinct, awkward tenderness of our limbs during the slow-elapsing moments that seep in our last embrace.

Heartbreak is only doing what doesn't work—heartbreak is all the subtle ways we lie to ourselves and stay small and in pain.

Love is doing what feels right and true and deeply honoring to even the most frightened parts of ourselves.

And so, we move from murky, merged co-dependence to the crisp clarity of independence.

Back, back, back.

We go back…and there is ocean in our lungs, but we don't drown.

No, we're done drowning in ourselves—and in each other.

Waves crash and froth at our feet. Renewal crests, fresh, clear water cleanses our raw, red, stinging skin.

We swim. We rise. We shake. We dance.

Our tears trickle into the deep blue of the sea and serve only to make it sweeter.

And, we are the same water. We came from the same place. We are beads on the same necklace.

I love you.

I am not ashamed of that.

I can't stop loving you. I've tried and failed.

I must try a new tactic.

Because we can love—*and* let go at the same time.

I think that's how we have to do it.

Hate damages our hearts. But freedom—freedom is the fresh gale of salty wind that takes us…

Back

Inside

Again.

Holy. It's peaceful and sanctified. Full of integrity. Spacious, but not empty. Spontaneous. Solid. Uncertain, but not terrified. There is grief, but no drowning. It's the ultimate uncovering of trust in ourselves, in the fragile whole of life itself. It's the dew that glistens on the grass of fresh possibilities.

Back, back, back…

To the truths that glitter in our own hearts.

To health—to the fiery sparks of our purpose.

May we stay and bask here for an eternity.

In this subtle clam shell of being born again, where the softness is so breathtaking and damn near unbearable at the same time.

This fragile space of love and loss—it's where the garden remembers it's a garden.

It's where the first tulip rises her red face in spring and sings to the sun.

It's where we begin to hear the whispers of the galaxy we are in.

It's where the whispers become not whispers anymore, but screams and deliciously unrelenting roars.

It's here.

With water, we separate…and I find myself again.

I find boundaries and clarity.

I love you—and that's okay.

Love can stay. That was the good part.

But, we can't be together. That was the bad part—the painful and horribly confusing part.

And, that's okay.

Back, back, back—to the tender beginning when I first met you.

Back even before that.

Back dipped into time…

Into me—and into the hot blood of the sun.

And words—so many words.

And painting,

And stars,

And life…

There is so much for me to plant in my garden.

There are so many ways I'm beginning to bloom.

Infinite petal rays shoot out from every inch of my skin.

I'm so ready to burst out of the thick mud of this sorrow that I have draped around me because I am scared to be without you. But, there is fire.

Yes. Fire is there too.

And so, the end becomes not the death of me…but my most brilliant blooming yet. Because I will make it so.

22.
I'm Not Sure I Can Forgive You, But I Can Forgive Myself

I've spent a thousand sleepless nights going over it and over it in my mind; retracing our steps, re-hashing our fights, replaying the harsh words we wish we never said.

How could you hurt me so much? How could I let you?

Bitterness steeped in my heart, like a sad tea. A little porcelain teacup full of bergamot and honey scented tears.

How could two people cause each other so much pain?

I still can't make sense of it, but maybe, I'm not supposed to.

For many moons, I cast you as an evil villain. A toxic person. Someone who took twisted pleasure in picking at other people's weaknesses. I cast myself as a helpless victim. A scared girl who didn't know any better.

But as time marches forward, the pages of my story turn yellow and begin to dissolve in the sunlight.

Without those tears in my eyes, I see differently. The veil of illusion lifts. I see that the truth lies well below the surface, miles beneath my carefully crafted version of events.

The truth is, *I played my part, too.*

I have to own my role in our love-spiked tragedy.

See, we were both broken and desperate, looking for someone to save us. The truth is, at the time, I needed our painful, fucked up relationship. I needed to learn about darkness. About power. About pain. I needed to learn to stand up for myself.

When I found my spine and walked away from you, I changed, forever.

I changed my fate.

I broke.

I fell down a canyon of truth.

And in breaking, in falling, I became myself.

My mask tore away like a dead leaf, revealing rawness and redness underneath; I screamed in horror, but I stepped into my skin. I stepped into who I really am.

As the sun rises today in a pale pink sky, I still don't know if I can forgive you. But, I can forgive myself. That is where I need to begin. A single flower of self-forgiveness falls softly around me, like a plush pink rose petal soaked in moonlight.

Through the softness of my own embrace, I begin to explore my gifts, my power, my beauty. Yet, I can't shake the shiver in my spine that tells me softly: what we shared was a gift. You taught me how *not* to love.

It didn't come with a shiny red bow; it came wrapped in poison. But as it turned out, that poison was medicine. It was the only thing that could have woken me up.

And brought me back to life again.

I hope it woke you up, too.

I hope it brought you back to life again.

23.
I'm Hungry For You

I need you to fill me up
In every way
In the dirtiest, grittiest way
In the sweetest, softest way
I need you to embrace me with your raw passion
I need to grip your skin with my fingertips
and bite your lips
and look into your eyes like the goddamn lioness I am
shock you with my gentleness
and make you mine again.
I'm hungry for you
your heart, your soul, just you, darlin'.
I'm hungry
my heart
needs to
touch
yours
not politely, honey.
wildly.
I need to crash into you
and let our cells collide
pulsating bodies that know so well how to dance together
I need to crash into you like a comet
and travel into nectar planes of existence
as you grab my face and kiss me absolutely everywhere.

I'm hungry, darlin'
and only you can satisfy my appetite
only you can quench this electric desire that courses through me
I'm hungry for you
I need to scream out
and lick
everything you are
as I fan the flames of
everything you want to be.

24.
Love Brings up Our Shit—Messy, Complex & Beautiful

I feel our love hatching, shedding its skin, and becoming beautiful again.

I'm surprised. I'm joyous. I'm scared.

Things between us have molted so much in the past few months, my love—I can barely keep up.

Our hands shook with fear back then, eyes glistening with tears, for we were about to let go of the way our palms and hearts melted together.

Then, we didn't let go of each other. But we *did* let go of something.

Change flashes like a camera. The bright light sparks something deep within—something golden and wild. For a moment, everything is illuminated, and we see things as they really are.

I love those striking moments of clarity.

Then, spots blink in our eyes. We are dizzy. We are uncertain, spinning together on the jagged, beautiful dance floor of life.

But we're smiling, trying to figure it all out, knowing that at some point we must surrender to the goddamn mystery.

Love is hard sometimes. It's like nothing I ever expected. And as I dare to drop the sheen of my high-gloss expectations, I feel naked and raw and free.

It's an odd sensation.

But I like it.

Because really, there's nothing like loving another to bring up all the shit inside us we didn't realize was still there.

Oh hello, trauma from three years ago. Oh hello, wounds from when I was 18. Oh hello, fantasies and illusions I forgot were informing my every move.

In some moments, I've felt deeply disappointed. For so long, I bought into the popular cultural narrative that when I "met the right person" everything would be perfect.

When that wasn't the case, I was convinced something was wrong. But in reality, I was left with the thudding realization that love isn't a magic wand, after all.

There is no glass slipper. No fairy tale.

We are still human—wounded and imperfect and beautiful. There is still conflict, fear, and pain. We still project unwanted parts of ourselves onto each other.

Our issues don't just evaporate.

And this isn't horrifying or hopeless. Love doesn't bring our shit to the surface to torture us, but so we can make sense of it and heal.

There are opportunities for learning so lush they could fill an entire library.

I am in awe that love actually is—not something to make us 100 percent happy at all times, or fulfill our every last whim—but a sweet vehicle of transformation.

A path to know ourselves better and see what an honor it is to be with a beloved.

To behold them on dark, stormy days and sunny ones, too.

Love can be more than happily ever after.

It can be the art of taking responsibility for ourselves in a new way.

It can be the art of becoming—of witnessing tears, success, disappointments, fear, laughter, and grief.

Yes, and doing that with another.

How messy. How complex. How simply beautiful.

My love, I'm glad I didn't give up a few months ago, when I was triggered like a bolt of lightning and just wanted to leave. I shut down.

My love, I'm glad you didn't give up a few months ago, when you were angry and thought we had pushed each other away for good.

Back then, our bond felt frayed beyond repair. My gosh, we can both be so stubborn—threatened by a hint of change, terrified by the mere prospect of compromise.

We've learned so much since then. We've grown. We've even—*gasp*—learned to compromise without compromising ourselves.

You stuck with me. I stuck with you.

Maybe we didn't know what the heck we were doing. But we sure were curious, weren't we?

Our love roared like wild winds, parting layers of sticky fabric sewn together.

Something old fell away.

You saw me. Of all things, that's what I needed. I needed to be known by you—for my insides to be decrypted bead by bead like a pearl necklace forged from the ocean herself.

I was naked and trembling—and in response, you were respectful and gentle.

You were naked and trembling—and in response, I was respectful and gentle.

We met each other with such tenderness. That meant the world to me.

Connection. It is where we become, where we have been hurt before, *and where we can be reborn.*

And so, as we lean in, as we whisper.

This delicious promise grows like something primal emerging from the sea—a messy turquoise beauty dripping wet, covered in salt.

This love renews itself, it takes work, it frustrates us, it challenges us, it gives us profound joy.

I'm so damn excited to keep walking on this adventure alongside you as grateful tears drench our cheeks.

Through our dedication, we've made the impossible possible:

I see that I can love you and not lose myself.

I can love you and have strong boundaries.

I can love you and love me.

Things I once thought were opposites are not actually opposites at all, but two beautiful parts that enrich each other endlessly.

Change flashes like a camera, the bright light sparks something from deep within—something golden and wild. For a moment, everything is illuminated, and we see things as they really are.

Our love is not perfect. It is even better—it's real.

It is an honor to know you.

It is an honor to show myself to you.

25.
Love Was Always Here: A Moment of Unforgettable Beauty

There it was, smack-dab in the middle of a gut-wrenching, soul-trying, tough week:

A soft, juicy moment where my heart was so overflowing with love, it just about brought me to my knees. But it was more than that.

It was deeper than any love I've ever known.

It was this strong sense of being comfortable in my skin. Feeling in control of my life. Feeling fulfilled in a fresh way.

More than anything, I felt, for the first time ever, that I am becoming the person I always wanted to be.

Tingles spread throughout my entire body, like soft butter. For once, my insides weren't tangled or twisted with panic or anxiety, but trusting in life, trusting in me.

My eyes misted with glorious tears of gratitude as a warm shiver travelled up my spine.

This moment smelled of rose petals and vanilla.

It felt like home.

It told me everything I needed to know.

Finally, I knew that all the pain was worth it. All the tears. All the uncertainty. All the heartbreak. All the failure.

Every goddamn sobbing struggle was worth it.

Because it led me here, to this moment, standing in a hot shower, feeling love ooze wildly from my heart.

My heart—my heart that has been so battered and broken and stepped on and taken advantage of. My heart that never dreamed of having the guts to speak her truth. My heart that never thought in million years she would stand for something real or succeed or feel remotely okay.

But, she found a single pearl of courage in a pool of teardrops, and began to rise up from the dead ashes of silence and abuse.

She's burning now—thumping away, *with passion, with imperfection, with truth.*

I nestle her softly in my arms, as a single salty tear rolls down my cheek, falling onto the wet shower floor with the tiniest little splash.

This moment was profound in its simplicity. Unforgettable in its tender beauty.

Could it be that this love was inside me all along? This peace, this serenity?

Yes.

It was always there.

Love was always there. Underneath the bullshit, the suffering, all the trials and tribulations—love was there—a single spark, just waiting to be ignited.

I was just too afraid to notice. Too afraid to set myself on fire and burn away everything I didn't need anymore.

I was too afraid to face pain. To face love. To face myself.

But I did.

And here I am—smiling in silence, as this moment slips through my soapy fingertips. Though this moment may fade and dissolve, it won't be forgotten. It will forever be a tiny diamond in my pocket, a reminder of the beauty woven into each of one our hearts, of the love that exists—even when we're hurting or suffering deeply.

Don't ever forget what's possible.

Look to the stars.

That same light is inside you. That beauty. That magic. That wonder. It all swirls around like a spiral galaxy, deep within your heart.

You are extraordinary; meant for extraordinary things.

Remember who you really are; what you're really here for.

Remember your truth, your mission, your juicy meaning.

Hold it close.

Come back to that feeling, because sometimes, that feeling is all we have.

It is the oil lamp that lights the way to your deepest, most refreshing fulfillment; the sweet magic that keeps you going. It is the love that brings you home.

26.
Maybe Love is Like a Firefly

"Maybe love is like this..." I think aloud, not finishing my sentence just yet, for my head falls into my lap—tears streaming down my cheeks, landing on my collarbone with a tiny splash.

I let 'em fall, for I sometimes think that with every tear we release, another layer is shed. I sometimes think that tears are like chisels, revealing the true diamonds of our beings.

So I dive in—sobbing, howling—a steady, salted rain falling from my eyes as my fingers clack to the rhythm of this familiar pain. I become the only thing I can in moments like this—*softer, more human, more vulnerable.*

Maybe love is like this...I think, finding that wistful thread once again, but wincing, still unable to finish the sentence just yet.

I simply hurt.

This is my current status—my heart: broken, again. Feeling lost and utterly alone again, but knowing I will be ultimately okay. Right now, though, the ache is fresh and raw.

Where did I go wrong? I wonder, unsure if I truly want to know the answer.

But as I drive home from town, my hands gripping the steering wheel, made hot from beams of golden sun, the car gently hugging the mountain curves—it comes to me.

Maybe love is like…*catching fireflies*. You know, the way we did when we were kids.

We fling open our doors and bolt outside on a summer evening, jars clanking in our hands, twilight giving way to a darkness that rolls out like a lush, star-studded carpet. The air is warm and the breeze is cool, caressing our cheeks as we run and play, our imaginations unstoppable, lit up like the moon.

We gasp with wonder as fireflies twinkle all around us, like a symphony of pure stardust. Our mouths hang open, as these glowing creatures embody everything that feels good. Everything ethereal, and pure, and innocent, and beautiful that exists in this world. The pristine, bouncing joy and simple *beingness* that often feels stolen from us, even if we can't articulate it just yet.

As we see the fireflies twinkling, we want to capture that magic— to feel it on our palms, for it to be planted deep inside us. We want to keep it. We need it to belong to us.

So, we catch fireflies and place their phosphorescent beauty in a jar, hoping to hold onto them forever, feeling blissful as they illuminate the darkness of our rooms, like little night lights.

But fireflies cannot survive in jars.

They will wilt, and wither, and die.

Their lights will go out.

They are meant to fly—to explore the sky, to glow so brightly, and be free.

Maybe love is like this.

We meet someone special, sparks fly—just like those lovely fireflies—and we are elated. We laugh 'til we cry, staying up late, talking about everything, and that same magic seeps into our veins again.

For the first time in what feels like forever, life just seems brighter. More fantastic. More vivid. It's all the things that this world often isn't—warm, and hopeful, and just plain sweet. Everything feels possible, expansive…

And it gives us permission to step into a flow that maybe we haven't, since we were children. There is wonder. Excitement. Shimmering effervescence. A delightful openness.

Our hearts become our eyes. We breathe in the elixir of connection and intimacy, brought back to life by soft touches and hungry kisses.

It's like waking up from a death we didn't know about—and suddenly we're able to see the beauty all around us again. It's that feeling of magic—magic not spoken, but felt, pulsing deep in our veins, as we shiver in sheer excitement.

And this magic ignites things deep inside us we had long forgotten about—desires, dreams, passions, what it is to throw caution to the wind and simply feel joy.

And we want to keep it. We want it to belong to us forever.

We want that initial spark—and what it ignites within us—to never, ever fade.

We want this person to always only ever be by our side.

Perhaps we would do anything to hold onto this feeling.

So we hold onto our love so tightly.

Too tightly.

We hold on fearfully, with wide eyes.

Because if love leaves us, maybe life will go back to how it was before—dull, blah, black and white, devoid of color, motion, and the jeweled radiance that drips down our chins.

Perhaps we fear that if we loosen our grip, our lover will slip through our fingertips like tiny grains of sand, and we will be abandoned, lost—alone again. Sad again. Empty again.

So, just like when we were kids, we desperately stuff the firefly—this magical, raw thing of our love—into a tiny glass jar, in our hearts.

But love can't survive like that, trapped behind thick, sturdy glass.

Nothing can.

It will suffocate, wither, and die. It will lie sad, unable to fly and fulfill its purpose.

But maybe love doesn't need to be like that at all.

Maybe the only way love can actually work is if *we are* the magic.

Our very own firefly.

And we get really awesome at soaring—sweeping past tall pine trees, our light glowing fiercely. We dig into life, what we're here to do, and fall love with the trembling nectar of existence itself.

And then, when the time is right—we meet another firefly, glowing just as brilliantly, flying just as joyously, living their purpose just as faithfully.

And then, the most beautiful thing happens—*we can fly together.*

Both of us are lit up. Both of us are filled with the unmistakable euphoria of who we really are. Both of us are cherishing what it is to soar in our own lives that we don't even think of stopping the deliciousness of the flight to hold tightly onto the other.

We are free, independent, content, and wild—yet supporting one another as we continue to rise.

Maybe this is the only way that love can actually work.

Maybe the biggest mistake we make is holding on too hard, coming from that shaky, scared place of desperation and lack.

We forget that we *are* the love. We are the magic.

It's not something to search for, it's something to *be*.

It is within us. Always.

We must cultivate our own blossoming—tending to the thirsty buds that glisten in our own hearts. We must nourish the sparkling embers of our own flames. And we must do this daily.

Because that magic we yearn for—we can have it anytime. We can be it anytime.

And when we attract another heart who is also whole and happy, lighting up the velvety night sky with all they've got—we will simply create more love. More beauty. More magic. More poetry.

For when a relationship is truly healthy, there is no drain. There is no sacrifice of our precious soul, or bleeding out of our energy. It is not toxic, fearful, co-dependent, or addictive.

It is simply abundant.

And we will feel the difference from the depths of our being.

By investing fully in our Selves—in our hearts, in our souls, in the burning passion that speaks to us in the most glorious whispers—*there is no losing*. We meet our own needs. We shine in our fullness. We become exactly who we are meant to be.

Because the more ignited, the more joyously, vividly ourselves we are—the more we will attract someone who can make our already awesome lives…a little sweeter.

And we will feel the difference.

It will feel so good and tingly—our souls will smile down to our toes.

It will be love, on our own terms.

Love, like never before.

A

Soaring

Love.

27.
Real Love is an Adventure. Real Love Takes Balls

I dab on perfume, slowing anointing my wrists with what smells like hope and cinnamon and the passion of melting candles and hot, delicious kisses, where our mouths meet and our souls soar.

Alive.

That's how I feel about what we're doing, my dear—the thing the world calls commitment.

Lately, we've been talking about marriage, creating a family, braiding our two separate lives into one. It gets scary sometimes, exciting as hell sometimes, and often, it evokes varying shades of the two.

But I want you to know something.

I'd like to call what we're doing an adventure instead. What do you think of that?

Because we are growing closer, exploring the fleshy tips of something we have not yet known. And it *is* an exploration, a voyage, a cross-country road trip.

There is music blasting and fresh, cool air that streams into our ears and messes up our hair.

And there are such big, goofy grins on both of our faces.

It's like biting into a luscious, red fruit—an exotic flavor we've not tasted yet. We try it together. Our chins drip happily, as we feed each other thick nectar slices with our warm, bare hands. Goosebumps cascade up and down the entirety of my spine as my breath mists, hot and hungry, with yours.

My love, it's in the way our skin feels together.

The way we write together, learn together, pray together, get inspired together, dive deep together, grow together—all of this, revealed in the foundation for something wide and flowing and great.

We are on an adventure.

And an adventure needs a few main ingredients.

First, we need bravery, the balls to do it—*to take the risk to love hard in the first place.*

Then, we need heaps of curiosity—the childlike wonder that is so powerful and pulsates within us with bright radiance, like confetti sparkling in the winter sunlight. This keeps us going.

And so, we do this—together.

Oh, shit—and as we get ready, as we bend our knees to jump, I forgot to mention the most important ingredient of all:

Faith.

I've never been good at trusting, but you are. Your faith sparkles and shines like a proud pearl you keep in your pocket at all times.

So I hope to learn from you about that quiet breath of surrender, and I hope to teach you things, too, my love. I hope to teach you about fire and femininity and feeling. I like the way we complement each other—similar, but different—bringing our own unique sets of strengths and weaknesses, wounds and wonders to the table.

But we are both adventurers. And we don't know what we're doing.

See, it's not that we're reckless. It's that, together, our laughter fills the sky. It's that we would die for one another.

But this love is not about death—it's about life.

Alive.

The taste crystallizes in my mouth, forming and blossoming into that which has no name. I struggle for it and then give up, surrendering into the bones of this experience instead.

Finally, an adventure companion!

That's what I really wanted all along.

So, our commitment widens and deepens—it's real. We will cover vast terrain. We will celebrate, show up for each other in beauty, in pain, when we are sick and sad, when we are joyous and ripe with inspiration, when it feels like nothing can go right. And every damn shade in between.

Yes, it's real.

But it's not heavy. It's nourishing. It ignites us both.

And there will be hard days, sure—but going into it expecting an adventure rather than a fairy tale changes everything.

To expect the gloriousness of mud under my fingernails rather than Cinderella's glass slippers…

Oh, yes.

I like the mud, the sweat, the challenge, the laughter, the joy, the exploration, the real.

And that's what this love is—real.

And I love the heart-balls it takes to make this leap together. I adore how right it feels. It smells like the radiance that comes when there is no more second-guessing, the gush of wisdom that rushes into our guts.

We can't tell the future. But the sun is warm on our cheeks, and we trust ourselves and each other.

We will take the leap together.

In the dazzling uncertainty of life, we will do this—and isn't that in itself astonishing?

For we are not weaving a fantasy that is glossy but essentially empty. We are two tender humans creating a reality that is imperfect and full, rich with meaning.

With chasing sunsets, talks of religion and philosophy, encouragement, arguments, compromises, fears, dancing around in the kitchen in our underwear, strenuous hikes up the side of jagged mountains, and the sheer and utter gratitude that we found each other in the first place.

Our love is not a fairy tale.

It's something so much better—*it's an adventure.*

So let's go on this adventure for the rest of our lives, fueled by the sheer and utter gratitude that we found each other in the first place.

28.
Sacred Sex: I Know Him & He Knows Me

Legs spread, I know him.

His hands, placed on the fleshy parts of my thighs, as he lowers himself down onto me.

I pant and bite my lip.

I know him.

Currents of electricity run up and down my body—hot and cold at once—red and magma, cool and blue.

He looks at me with no effort, only the care that oozes naturally from the potency of his gaze, locked on mine.

And mine on him.

He knows me.

This is delicious beyond belief—I think, as he draws me closer to him, tears like pearls destined to pour out of both our eyes.

He doesn't touch me like I am marble—no, he touches me with reverence, but with the distinct knowledge that I am real and solid. Wild and here.

A tigress, unfolding in his arms.

And I am.

And in these moments—I let go completely.

And he is a healer. I trust him that much.

I surrender completely—my body melts and reforms, liquid then solid.

Then gold,

Trembling and smiling

What I know is this—

I know him.

And he knows me.

That's why it's so good. That's why this is different.

Passionate, but careful—*full of care*—heart leads the way for bodies to crash and cascade on each other like waterfalls, mixing our waters to form a new, rich, expansive sea.

Soul drips to form togetherness.

I am home.

This is it.

I arch my back in ecstasy as he kisses my neck, tattooing his love into me with his lips—bedazzling me invisibly, but in this palpable way that lights me up.

The divine is alive, awake in him.

It is so beautiful, I could weep —

Instead I lay back, as he enters me, slowly, with all his focus on feeling, on my body, on decoding what my face says.

I relax deeply, spreading like silk to allow him inside.

I look at him and do this novel thing — I let myself be loved.

Thoroughly.

Reverently.

I let myself be seen, for all my wildness and wounds and all that has made me wise and tough, soft, strong, and interesting.

And I love him.

His love pours into me, bright white and pure — I glisten.

He glistens.

Sweat becomes art, then all the grit becomes diamonds.

In this, an unspoken bond is formed.

29.
The Art of Loving Loneliness.

It is 7 p.m. The air is stagnant and heavy, breezeless, begging for rain. The trees are still and thirsty. My temples throb with anticipation and a feeling of anxiety.

It is 7 p.m. The loneliness is so big I swear it could swallow me whole.

Were evenings always this long, this drawn-out, this empty?

Were the moments always stretched so thin, a frayed eternity packed in a single second?

My voice is low, a hoarse whisper, as I ask these questions aloud, in increasingly begging tones. The tears come now, as darkness slowly falls on the horizon, like a curtain—and I long for the scraping gravel sound of your car pulling up. Then my heart could do happy flip-flops, instead of throbbing with this lead-like heaviness.

My skin seems to stretch out, as though it's waiting for your kisses, for every ounce of me remembers the tender, salty touch of your lips.

I am hungry. Not for food. After all, I just ate dinner, but for love—*your love*. I am hungry to be touched by your hands and loved by your lips. It is a hunger I walk around with daily. It has embossed my face, it's a parched spot in my throat—a deep hunger I cannot satiate.

It's 7 p.m. Saturday night. I wish we could be together at the river having a picnic, talking about everything, and eating dried mangoes.

I look down at my phone, like maybe it's an oracle, like it could give me all the answers—searching. Searching. I search for something. But I come up with nothing. Just wishing I had the courage to text you the three words that seem like the scariest things to admit to myself, let alone to you—*I miss you.*

But I can't do that.

Instead, I slip into a bubble bath, the steam and lavender oil eating away a big chunk of this gaping feeling in my chest, like there's a giant crater where you used to be.

Because, I think, as the bubbles reach up to my chin, if I did reach out, I would want it to be because I love you. Not just because I'm lonely.

And do I know the difference yet?

Not quite.

So silence sings between us, save for the few texts of arranging when you'll pick up your things. And I really thought this parting of ways would be so much easier. I didn't think it would hurt this much.

It's all the things my mind can't figure out. It's all the why's and how's and wondering—will it maybe work out at some point? It's all the nagging questions and non-answers that drive me nuts.

A neighbor knocks on my door, the rhythmic sound jolts me out of my thought-filled reverie, but I don't answer.

I'm fresh out of the bath, naked, crying on the bed, and I don't want anyone to see me. I don't want to speak, for my lips can't move, only my fingers reach to type. I hide in these words like they are the thick, soft bosom of a nurturing mother.

I'm so lonely, but I need to find my way through this.

That's the truth.

My mind races again, cycling predictably—did I give up too easily? What happened between us? Why did everything spoil and turn sour?

But the thoughts lead nowhere.

I don't want to think.

I want to simply be.

So I breathe in, and do what feels so brave—I don't call you. I don't call anyone. I could, *but I know that's not what I need.*

I expand into this thing called loneliness.

Slowly, awkwardly, one inch at a time, I explore the vastness of her edges. And as I do, I realize she isn't so scary. She's quiet, oddly peaceful, full of these words, ripe with fruits of fragrant possibility, and little sparks of all the things I didn't know I could do...

I expand into loneliness. I steep in her, like tea.

The result is breathtaking. Shocking, too.

I expect it to feel terrible, upsetting, and harsh, like getting my eyebrows waxed—but I feel held. Courage blooms from the growing softness in my heart. Plumes of fire are born of plush tenderness. My whole body relaxes, for I didn't realize how tired I was.

I face tonight alone.

And I didn't know I was so scared to be alone, but maybe we all are sometimes—and that's okay. Let us dive right into the fear. Let us not avoid it, because that only gives it power. And as always, once we face fear, even by just voicing it—it becomes infinitely less scary.

I sit boldly in the lap of this alone—unfolding into her, like a lotus flower blooming one petal at a time.

Stillness comes over me.

I melt deeper. My bones become silk. And even though in moments my heart still beats so hard it feels like it could smash into smithereens—I find that I do this alone rather well. I'm not bad at being alone. I just rarely give myself the chance to practice.

So practice I do.

I plunge into this spaciousness—to explore the mystery of me…

All the hot, spinning galaxies I am, all the truths and stories and heartbreaks that are packed inside me. And it feels empowering.

I navigate what felt impossible just moments ago…I rest in the arms of loneliness.

Immense freedom comes over me, in a shiver, in a feeling of excitement and expansion.

Yes. There is immense freedom in this.

Self-reverence.

Trust.

Celebration.

Loneliness wraps around me like a robe. And it is not empty or barren—it becomes sacred. Luscious in its own, strange wonderful way.

"This time is just for you," loneliness whispers.

"This time is just for me," I repeat, the words dripping into me like a prayer. It is my space to heal. To feel. To be.

Maybe this is the thing I've fought so hard for—to simply sit with myself. And feel peace in the midst of chaos and "not knowing" that is life.

For is that not life-changing in itself?

And on this night that I thought would spread before me, long and endless—the most unexpected thing happens—I fall in love with loneliness.

I part her veil, and she slips inside of me.

"Tell me all your secrets," I beg. But she is quiet. There are no questions. There are no answers. There is just this. The royal weightlessness of being. I paint upon her canvas with the shakiness of my breath.

I become more quiet.

For once, I don't need to do a thing.

There is nothing to figure out. Struggle becomes irrelevant.

Loneliness changes faces; she becomes not spikes, not a monstrous entity, not the thing I've tried so hard to avoid—but a safe place to rest my weary heart.

She becomes sacred space. A net of holiness.

She becomes a deepened connection with myself. For it is only from this satiated place of soul-deep self-connection that I can connect with others in a healthy way.

I kiss loneliness, and she is not sharp or bitter. She is not poison. She is soft, smelling of a thousand pink roses picked from my mother's garden. She is sweetness. The luscious pause I didn't know I needed to take.

And on this night, I fall in love with loneliness.

She becomes the cornerstone of my practice.

I open to receive her blessings, even the sadness.

And I am left speechless.

I don't need anyone to fill this space. I don't need anyone to fill the hole inside of me. I need not even fill it with my own worries. It is mine to bask in. To heal into. And even, to love.

Silence reigns. Simplicity just is. Freedom drips everywhere.

I am just here, with my Self.

Everything is now. And none of my problems or pains are fixed, but I don't need them to be…

Because this. Just this.

Fresh joy permeates.

And I am left speechless.

This aloneness is perfect in a way that nothing ever has been.

It is pure, untouchable by logic or mind.

It is art.

It is love…

The song of silent solitude draped graciously in my heart.

30.
To My Future Love—When We Finally Meet, Let's Take it Slow

Maybe we have both rushed things in the past—I know I have tumbled foolishly into love far too many times.

My heart is tender—she is real, and she can't take fast-paced, whirlwind romance disasters anymore, so I have one request for you, sweet and wild mystery man of my future...

Let's take it slow. One breath at a time. One date at a time. One sip of spicy red wine blooming on our tongues like roses at a time.

Be patient with me. I'll be patient with you.

Let's exhale, allowing this to unfold like a yard of tangerine silk fabric—unveiling itself, layer by layer, in its own perfect time—letting it bud, then blossom, just as it is meant to.

Good things aren't meant to be rushed, and what is destined to exist between us is like a chocolate soufflé—it needs time to rise and settle into its *truest, most delicious form.*

I want to talk. I want to get to know you, to see the man behind all the things you do, to sneak peaks at little cake slices and slivers of your juicy heart. I want to see if our hearts dance to the same electric beats, if our souls are both on a ballsy quest to seek truth and adventure thirstily through life.

I don't want this unless you fit me like a glove.

I want to be certain.

Because when our lips lock in a beautiful first kiss outside—the grass glowing neon green from the perfect amount of rain and sunshine, fireflies lighting up the night with specks of magic—I want to be ready.

I want our bodies to draw together like magnets, knowing it's right, relaxing into the sublime rightness, savoring it vividly.

I want our feet to get wet on the dewy grass, toes muddy, hearts smiling, falling asleep underneath an ancient oak tree, talking about the moon, philosophy, religion, heartbreak and truth as twilight falls upon us like a starry blanket and tucks us into each other's arms.

Let's go deep—but *slowly*. Very slowly, like a striptease of two hearts, like a sunrise revealing her colors, one apricot-drenched cloud at a time.

Let us unpeel this love with care, with tenderness, letting it ripen like a plump, blushing raspberry.

And when our hearts are ready, when the leaves of this love are crisp and emerald green, we will rip it off the branch carefully, eagerly, and we will share the berry and the burden equally— cherishing it, savoring it with wild hunger, forever.

I want us to be best friends and then lovers, letting each other into our secret worlds a little at a time, revealing small truths like whispered teasers to movies, then finally unveiling the whole screenplay when the curtain goes up and our hearts are buck naked beneath the moon-struck sky.

I want us to know it's right. To feel it in our guts—a fact, a truth, a reality—not a fantasy, not a question.

I don't want to guess.

I don't want to stretch myself to make us fit—and I won't be someone else to make you happy.

I've done that too many times and ended up exhausted, thin, hollow and broken from pretending—from bending and from forcing two heart pieces together that almost fit, but just don't, not quite.

I want to be me, and I want you to be you. No masks. No pretenses. No bullshit.

I want us to fit naturally, organically.

I want to take you apart like a puzzle. Take me apart too—yes, when it's time—unwrap every inch of me like a present, and I'll show you everything I hide from the eyes of the world. I'll show you the scratches on my soul, the wounds on my heart, the spicy ginger-like flavors of my feisty mind.

I'm not ashamed of my darkness, my grittiness, my roarin' femininity, and I want you to know exactly what you're getting yourself into...

I want you to witness the shockwaves of my lightning-like intensity. I want my wild flames to make you weak in the knees—to spark a glittering glint in your eager eyes and an accelerated heart rate in your chest as a wicked smile spreads across your mouth, telling me that you won't be able to keep your hands off me.

No man has ever been able to handle me—but I know *you* can.

You won't back down from a challenge, will you darlin'?

Well, I'm your challenge. I'm your tornado. I'm not the flimsy foam on top of your latte—no, I'm the espresso beans grinding, flying around with electric pulses and pouring into your bloodstream, jolting you the fuck awake.

Don't worry, I will love your raw fire, too. Your gentle fierceness. Your strong, determined mind. And I will not be afraid of your oozing masculinity—I will love it, cherish it, eat it up by the spoonful and appreciate you for *all you are.*

We will excitedly weave our lives slowly together—thread by thread, seam by precious seam—because you are a man who doesn't shy away from the responsibility of having kids, starting a beautiful family, being an open-hearted warrior. You will be up for making this *real*.

You won't turn away, you will be electrified by it all.

You will be my warrior, my equal, my fellow adventurer and passionate explorer of life, and I will love you fiercely. I will not hold back the petals of my messy heart from you. I will let you in—slowly, but truly—and I will set you free with every trace of my fingertips along the ridges of your back.

We will make the world more beautiful together, we will make art every time we kiss.

I will paint you to life in the sleepy thickets of my dreams, with the vivid watercolors of my tears.

I can't wait to meet you.

But I'm not ready—yet. Maybe you aren't either.

I'm still rising from the ashes of my pain, I'm finding confidence, my purpose, my truth—and I'm just starting to wake up and realize that I deserve an astounding, amazing, toe-curling, comfortable as my favorite sweater, wild as the wind, *beautiful love.*

And I know you're out there. *I can feel you.*

I'm right here—but I'm not ready, not just yet.

I need time to heal, space to grow and bloom into the bad-ass woman you will someday love.

I need to become whole.

And when the time comes, we'll recognize each other instantly. I know we will.

Our hearts are both flames—spirits written in stardust, sealed with gritty truth, souls both longing for something deeper, something more than an ordinary love.

Until then, I'm working on me. I hope you're tending gently to your heart's needs too.

Be ready for me.

I'm a storm, so it's a good thing you like the rain.

I'll appear to you like a golden streak of lightning in the velvety midnight sky. I'll appear to you, when you least expect it.

Watch for me. Wait for me.

When our lips meet, our hearts will exhale, our mouths will smile, and the air will be filled with the satisfied sighs of two souls finally finding their mates.

It won't be perfect, but *it will be right.*

Be patient with me.

I'll be patient with you.

This will be the love we've always longed for, the love we almost stopped believing in.

We will finally know it's real.

Until then, my love…

31.
With You, I Feel Like Fire

I want to fuck your soul
He told me
In the soft silence
Of dawn
Tucked away
In a warm bed
In his warm arms
Bodies sweaty
Pressed together
We speak through kisses *only*
And hold each other's gaze
For a million moments
That shatter us away from the mundane
Particles of life float around us, like dust
Frozen in space
You and me, baby.

There is nothing else
There is *no thinking allowed*
Only feelings
That gush over our skin
And give us goosebumps
As we shudder from the sheer power of it all
Feeling a little ashamed to care so deeply
To feel so much

Your Broken Heart is Art

When you look at me
When I look at you
But we don't hide from the intensity
We welcome it
Eyes locked
Mouths moving
Fumbling for more kisses
To dive deeper
To see you
To show you *me*.

Your gaze is unmovable
Electricity flickers
On our skin
And deep within
It touches our hearts
Soaks our souls
It is magic
And all the molten things I used to be afraid of
Like not hiding
Or guarding my heart like it's a goddamn prison
Renewal crests like a wave
Openness is here.

Words float to the surface
They add texture and meaning
With your gaze locked on mine
I smile
I feel like fire

I want to fuck your soul
I will take your breath away
And be a gust of wind
That knocks you back
Inside
To the mysteries
You forgot about
That are still there
And always will remain.

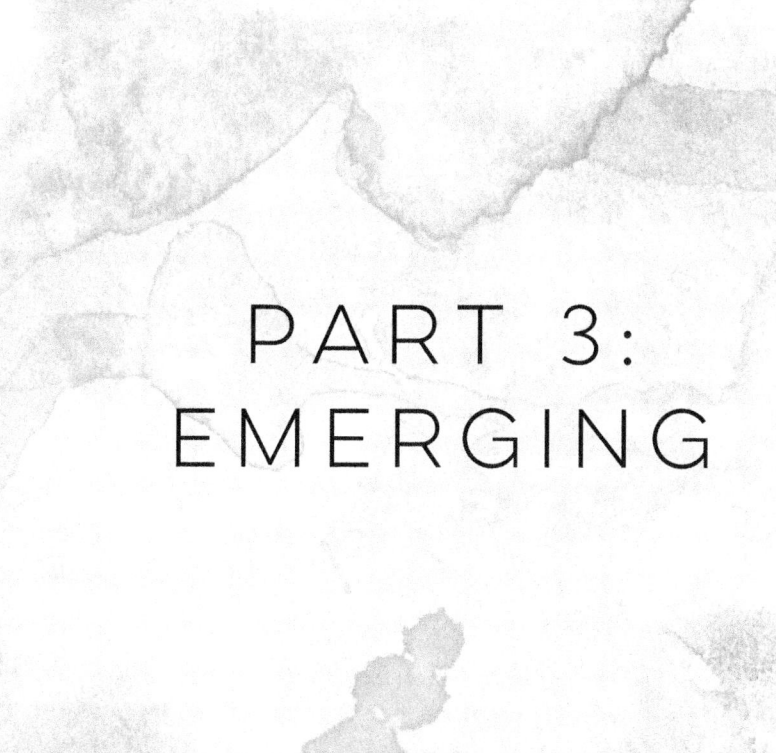

PART 3: EMERGING

32.
A Sweet Love Letter for Your Tired & Broken Heart

Hey, beautiful.

I know that you may not feel beautiful right now. Shit, I've been there.

Maybe you feel exhausted, freakin' angry, or utterly alone. Maybe you're hurting like hell or confused.

Maybe your heart has been freshly broken and you're crying on the bathroom floor.

I hear you.

I hear you in the whispers, in the shadows, in the streams of cool winter sunlight that spill in through my windowsill.

And I know—life can be tough and terrible, shocking, and really scary sometimes.

But in the dips and hollows of it all, in the thundering darkness of trauma and pain, in all the awful, toxic things we can be told—I hate that we can come to think we are worth *nothing.*

That our value has vanished.

That our power, our ability to love, create, and enjoy has been taken by the hands of those who could never even see us in the first place.

And yet, we yearn to be seen. To be witnessed in all of our glittery, gritty, messy, sweet glory.

So, can I tell you something?

I see you—for more than you wounds.

I see beyond the edges of your brokenness, past the valleys of the limits you've come to believe.

I know that your wounds are a part of you, mine are a part of me, too—in a way, they spark spirit to create wonder and all of the fresh, emerald growth that happens from the ache.

But it is not easy to feel broken.

And I want to hold space for you as wise, wild, and wonderful women did for me.

I see that, yes, you are hurting. I see the ache, and honor it so fiercely.

I see all of that. And more.

Because even in your tears, I can still taste your wisdom—the brilliance that emanates out of you when you're not even trying.

I see your softness that is so powerful.

I see your beauty.

Your Broken Heart is Art

I see your strength and resilience.

I see your passion.

I see the delicious depths to which you dive and shimmy and feel.

I see all the creativity that pours out of you.

Your brokenness is but one beat in an entire melody—you are so much more.

And I want to reflect wholeness back to you. Because in spite of it all, you *are* still whole. You are still fantastic and so brave.

You are setting yourself free.

Let the layers peel back—let something fresh gush forth from the pain.

You have so much to offer, simply by being who you are.

Please don't hide.

Take up space,

Whenever you're ready—that's when it's time.

I want you to know that you are seen.

'Cause I know it can feel hopeless sometimes, empty and impossible.

This life can feel cruel.

But I see that flicker of juicy life in your eyes. I see a smile that speaks of curiosity and fire.

I see you.

And I know, it's hard to be a woman in this world. It's hard to have the guts to rise in the face of it all. It's hard to speak up, to be soft, to be real, to be ourselves.

It's hard to do that, when we feel like the world shuts us down. Yet, we are called to do it anyway.

You hear the call reverberating deep in your bones, don't you?

'Cause you are like the earth.

You crack, you open, you light up in brilliant color and lose all of your leaves, you get quiet with the snow, then you warm up, you flower and bloom, you get wonderfully hot and spicy—and do it all over again.

You are like the earth. That grounded. That vast. That sensual.

You are able to hold so much—the fire and possibility, the icy shock of loss, the muddy rivers of grief, the bitter canyons of pain, the fields of delicious love, and the sweet, dewy fragrance of hope.

I see you.

I see the strength and vulnerability of your big, open heart.

Your Broken Heart is Art

I see the unwavering wonder of your spirit.

I want you to know that you matter, even when you don't think you do.

Your wounds may shape you, yes—but I promise they don't have to define you.

Because,

Beneath the pain,

Even in the wreckage,

Is satin treasure.

A draped and heavenly paradise.

And,

I want you to know that you matter, even when you don't think you do.

33.
An Open Letter to Those Who Love Someone Struggling With PTSD or Trauma

Because I know trauma intimately, I forget that some people don't.

And I would never wish that thundering darkness on anyone.

But I hate feeling misunderstood. I think many of us do.

To most people, I look fine—maybe I seem a bit awkward in moments—and now, after many years of hard inner work, I *am* fine. I feel like myself. I feel real and whole, intact—stitched together again.

But there are still stories that lie under the surface of my skin.

The ache goes away gradually, it lessens in intensity, but there are fractions and fissures, shadows and echoes that remain. It's a constant work in progress, and I am okay with that.

There's even beauty in it.

But unless it's happened to you, I don't think you can fathom what it is to be shattered. To be numb, floating outside your body, and unable to come home to yourself because you are so afraid—afraid of the feelings that are so big.

Sorrow, shame, anger, rage, and panic swirl inside, and you seem to suffocate as you struggle not to drown in their depths. And these depths seem to go on and on, into the inky sapphire of midnight.

Everything becomes tinged with danger. Nothing feels trustworthy. Safety is nowhere to be found. Much is seen through the lens of the past, of what happened.

Life becomes hard. So very hard.

Things that used to feel easy can feel impossible. Leaving the house can feel impossible. Simple things like going to the store or looking someone in the eye feel scary beyond words. Threat, threat—everywhere. Our bodies might shake, even in stillness, for we are constantly on red alert. Our bodies may feel unable to fully relax, and vigilance becomes our best friend.

We may retreat from the world, isolate, wonder what the hell is wrong with us, or fear we're crazy (*P.S. we're not*). We might react strongly to loud noises or sudden movements. We may react strongly to many things, because we so badly fear being hurt or violated again.

It's intense.

I don't dive into these depths to taste the pain—I've already tasted it. It is my past, no longer my present, and not my future. But these experiences will always be a part of me. They shaped me. And I know there is wisdom in that.

I know I cannot contribute to the silence on this topic. I want to honor the pain that so many of us go through.

Now, I wish for PTSD and trauma to be common knowledge. Normalized. No longer stigmatized. Understood by those who have been to the darkness and those who have not. Honored by those who love survivors, phoenixes, and fighters.

Remember these things if you love someone healing from trauma, PTSD, or abuse. Know that your support can mean the world.

Don't say we should be healed already. It's a process. Honor that it can hurt so much.

Don't tell us what we need. We know.

Don't say that we shouldn't feel this way. Because it makes complete sense that we do.

In a matter of mere moments, our lives were turned upside down. We were left confused, our eyes wide with shock, trying to make sense of it all. And it may still not make sense.

Trauma rocks our world. It shakes us to the core.

We feel it in our bodies. Our hearts. Our skin. Our nervous systems, which may never be the same again.

Even when we start the healing, it takes time. There is no rush. There is all the time we need to heal.

Because *time* is what we didn't have when trauma happened and we couldn't take it in. There was no time. The clock sped up and stood still, all at once. We could not integrate the experience.

Now, our bodies speak to us in sensations that we slowly learn how to read.

We are not pathology.

We are not bad or ugly or wrong or weak.

We are healing.

And sometimes our nervous systems get raw and flash with signals that tell us to run or freeze or fight.

But precisely because we have been to the depths, swum in rivers of ancient grief, and climbed out of hollow, terrible places with grit and courage and even just a tiny flame of hope...

We change. We crack open—never to be the same. In the crevices of the brokenness, we are born again. We can choose that.

It's not easy. It's messy. It's hard to describe.

So don't you dare think that we are fragile little things. Don't look at us with pity in your eyes.

We are tender, but oh so strong.

And we know. We know things you can't imagine.

We may even come out of this experience different in truly remarkable ways—because it's not just post-traumatic stress, it's also post-traumatic growth, post-traumatic breakthroughs, post-traumatic love, post-traumatic sweetness, post-traumatic badassery, post-traumatic wisdom.

In the death of it all, there can be a fragrant budding of fresh, tender life.

Maybe we will find a new purpose. Dedicate to an old dream.

Maybe we will soften. Meet God. Taste the vast reservoir of our resiliency and strength. Find beauty and meaning in the simple things—like a cup of tea with a loved one while watching a yellow-tinged leaf dance into a puddle.

Maybe we will find dancing or painting or writing or art or science—and never understand how we could have lived or breathed without such soulful medicine.

Maybe we will learn to reach out for help, and see that even though there is such darkness and cruelty in this world, there is also such softness and kindness.

Maybe we will know joy again, in ways that sizzle like magnolia buds in early spring and take us over the way pain used to.

Maybe we will learn how luscious it is to care for ourselves so tenderly.

We will never be the same, see. When the cracks and crevices formed, they changed us. We fought and we surrendered.

And it isn't shiny, this process. It's messy as hell. It's damn beautiful. It's so real.

But, understand. Understand the immense feelings. The fear and chaos. The bone-deep exhaustion we may still feel.

Understand that there were terrifying things—and people—beyond our control.

Support us with love as we come home to our bodies again. Support us with gentleness as we find the rhythm of our voices again.

Do not silence our stories when we are ready to speak.

Offer us respect. Touch us with care. Understand the ways that we still may ache, even years or decades later.

Listen to our thoughts, our feelings, our views.

See us. See the strength we gathered in the depths. See the treasures we found when we thought we were buried in darkness.

Know the courage that got us through.

34.
For the Free-Spirited Females With Fiercely Sensitive Hearts

This is for the gentle goddesses with watery, empathic hearts, who ooze with oodles of compassion, eager to soothe another's suffering.

This is for the luscious ladies with restless spirits who can't stay in one place for long, because our souls are winged, always longing for adventure.

Yes, this is just for us:

The free-spirited females with fiercely sensitive hearts.

We are a balmy breeze, casually caressing arms lovingly, suddenly here, suddenly there, then suddenly gone.

We are a thousand grains of precious pink sand, slowly slipping through soft fingertips, one by one.

We can never be contained because we aren't meant to be.

We are born to ride the wild winds of passion, surf the turbulent oceans of despair, and relentlessly explore the great vastness of this crazy world—until our bodies collapse in ecstatic exhaustion.

We understand deeply that life is a heartbreakingly beautiful series of goodbyes, hellos, triumphs and disappointments and we feel most alive in the midst of transformation, courageously shedding our old skin to be birthed again, raw and new.

We are well-versed in letting go, able to boldly exhale and swiftly set fire to the past, painstakingly gathering the ashen wisdom to build a more abundant future.

We are phoenixes, falcons, eagles and butterflies.

We are light and airy, yet never lacking depth.

We are carefree and sparkly, but our effervescence actually emanates from caring so deeply, from feeling the world's pain, happiness, love, sadness and struggle wildly pulsate within our chests, day in and day out.

We are spongy emotional barometers, picking up on another's mood immediately, sensing anxiety, anger, grief, frustration and jealousy. Feeling it so damn intensely that we sometimes suffocate.

We crave alone time, solo adventures, secret places and quiet spaces because the world can seem so scary and overwhelming that we wonder if it could, in fact, swallow us entirely in one single gulp.

We love wholly, compassionately and completely—but never possessively.

We have to fly away sometimes, darting out in the velvety black of night because we know that by setting ourselves free, we can set others free too.

We deeply respect our femininity, listening closely to the whispering wisdom of our intuition, the mystical murmurs of our ancestors and the primal pulse of nature.

We feel most alive outside, wings fully spanned, feeling the firm ground beneath our feet, welcoming the fiercest winds to whirl through our wispy hair.

We are fierce warriors, forces to be reckoned with—precisely because we are so sensitive.

My gentle and free-spirited sisters, I hear your feathery roar.

Let us spread our wings and soar.

Let us fly long and fast and hard.

Let us fly unapologetically.

Into the incredible lives we are meant to live.

Let us vow now.

To never turn our backs on the wise contents.

Of our fabulously free-spirited.

And fantastically sensitive souls.

35.
Freedom: Just You, Your Breath & the Universe

Slow.

Down.

Freedom is not found in a fight-or-flight response,
the fast-paced ways we live our lives.

It is not found in perfection.
It is not found in repeating the same old patterns until we die.
It is not found in finally being liked by everyone.
It is not found in doing more, more, more until our bodies ache.
It is not found at the mall, next to the hats, gloves, and scarves.

Freedom is subtle and gigantic at the very same time.
So big, so softly sweet, so soaring you might miss it.

You might not feel it filling your lungs,
roaring to quench that ancient thirst,
the hunger you were born with.

Freedom is found in your heart.
In those rare, delicious moments of *stillness*,
when everything drips out,
and you sit
listening, listening

to the precious pulse of the universe herself.

And she is loud.
She is steady.
Hold your ear to the earth like she's a shell
and listen.

Freedom is subtle.

It is found in spaces between anger, hollowness, fear, shame,
and doubt.
And we must feel our feelings.
When we do, they break up,
and their consistency changes
from rock-hard salt
to water.
And you can move.
You can swim
and feel
and find the way
in the ripples of each wave.

You melt into the fabric of life itself,
being stitched and remade,
with each tear and heartbreak and possibility and joy.

Freedom.
It is found in the moments
when we are alone
and can face
ourselves.

Your Broken Heart is Art

There is no distraction.
There is just you,
your breath,
the universe,
and
God.

And there is nowhere to hide.
And you're so glad.
Because you wouldn't dream of it.

Freedom
can bring tears,
the courage to look at the tender humanness we are, you are, I am.
As you touch your own cheek gently, lovingly.
As you dare to *not* look away.

Freedom
is in the ability to face
the death of the old
and be dazzled
by the fresh, sweet blossoming
of
the new.

36.
My Heart Said to Be Gentle. So I Listened

It happened last night, between the manic, whirling gusts of icy-cold wind.

A feathery little magic moment landed right onto the exhausted, dewy leaves of my soul.

It shook me up, kissed my lips sweetly, and left me breathless.

I didn't know it yet, but this little magic moment would reveal itself as a long-awaited answer to a burning-hot question of mine:

Why does working on myself hurt so fucking much?

Wait…

Let's unwrap the caramel-candy deliciousness of this moment slowly.

I was buried deep under my blankets, drinking decaf tea, watching Netflix.

I thoughtlessly twirled my hair and suddenly my hands discovered these huge nest-like knots hanging near the nape of my neck.

Annoyed and impatient, I grabbed a hairbrush, ready to wage war against my wavy, tangled tresses.

But, I stopped.

My heart told me to stop.

She said: *Please don't wield your brush like a reckless sword, fiercely battling the out-of-control wheat field in your hair.*

She said: *Be gentle. Comb through each strand lovingly, like a spatula slowly stirring luscious melted milk chocolate.*

I listened.

And licked my lips a little.

I took small sections of my naughty, knotted hair, and did as my heart instructed.

I didn't rush, or pull or push.

I took it one tangle at a time, one strand at a time.

I breathed in and I knew:

This is exactly how I need to work on myself.

Gently, supportively, kindly, lovingly, patiently.

This is the path to true transformation.

I forget.

Because it can feel so much easier to work on myself recklessly, violently, carelessly.

To criticize and chastise my wounds while I'm slogging through shit.

To become disgusted and ashamed as I confront the dark, slimy demons in my heart.

No more.

Because when I look with soft, caring eyes, I see that the shit is actually just fear and those demons in my heart are actually just scared little girls, shaking and shivering in the freezing cold winter wind.

They need love, not criticism.

They need so much love. And a thousand cups of chamomile tea. And several hundred spoonfuls of Nutella.

So—from now on, I vow:

If I am to work on myself, then I must do it kindly.

Yes!

I must go slowly and patiently as I'm peeling back layers and peering into my juicy soul.

I must wrap my wounds in soft, silky blankets while I'm dredging up clunky old suitcases stuffed with grief.

I must hug my heart when she's breaking, beating so fast, and being shy.

I must do all this and more—because I need my own love and support so fucking badly when I'm working hard on healing and transforming myself.

Because that kind of unconditional love and unwavering support is the most important work of all.

Listen to your heart.

What does she say?

What does she whisper in rhythm with her soulful beats?

Listen to your heart.

She's wicked wise.

37.
Pain & Difficulty Give You Wings

When things fall apart
The golden wings of opportunity swoop down
To guide you.

Because now's your chance to fly
To fucking soar.
To change direction.
To go exactly where you want, for a change.

Yes.

Or—

You can continue grasping for the already broken pieces.
You can continue reaching out for the beautiful, but empty illusions.
You can continue pouring energy into the blackholes of distraction.

Please don't.

Things fall apart for a reason.
Things collapse for a reason.
Things go up in flames for a reason.
 They have to be destroyed.

Your Broken Heart is Art

They have to be obliterated.
They have to shatter completely.

Because then
And only then
Can we make way for the really beautiful things.

Yes.

Destruction is flawless.
It's perfect.
The ruthlessness only adds to its beauty.

And, yes.
I know.
It hurts like hell to watch it all fall away.

But—

Don't second-guess it.
Don't make excuses.
Don't fight it.

It's brilliant.
And, it need not be so painful.
Because the destruction is molding us into ourselves.

Look!
Can you see the little roots underneath the wreckage?

Bright with hope.
Glowing with possibility.
Twinkling with magic.

What makes these stubby roots so sparkly?
We do.

Our broken hearts and hurt feelings are the perfect fertilizer for transformation.
Because real growth needs to be watered by the hardships of the past.

So, let us be deeply thankful for difficulty and pain.
They open our eyes.
Then our hearts.

They give us wings,
So we can go *exactly* where we want, for a change.

38.
Silence Speaks. Listen.

The silence speaks, I swear it does—
Of adventures to be had
Secrets to be untangled
Sweet yearning to be tasted
And
Ecstasy so subtle
It trembles in your belly
And reverberates
Through. Your. Heart.
It pierces through every wall that ever was.
Sit in a stream of silence
Stare at like the stars on a clear night
Let it speak
In foreign tongues
Your body knows
So well.
Listen…
Fall into the silence.
Surrender like a bird
To the sapphire sky
Let
Go.
Let the seafoam wash over you
Like waves
Taking you to places inside

Beautiful and terrifying
Messy and sweet
And real.
Find yourself again
Emerging
In silence
Embrace
In a breath full of mystery
Who you are. Who you were. Who you aren't. Who you wanted to be.
Let it all wash over you.
Let. Go.
As tears drip gratefully
Down to your toes.

39.
Sit Courageously in the Fires of Your Struggle

Setbacks aren't setbacks, they're spring-forwards. Things fall apart because they sucked to begin with. We aren't broken; we're shedding old, constricting skin.

We have to let ourselves unravel like spools of thread, splatter onto the dirty sidewalk, and crack wide open.

Sweat, bleed, cry, and scream; let your wounds drip and ooze like thick raindrops.

Once we're nice and raw, we can gently remove the scarves of worthlessness and self-hatred covering our delicious souls.

Whoosh!

What's inside?

Look deeper.

What's underneath our aching skin?

Pain; yes, there's pain. There is always pain. We need to get comfortable with discomfort and let each salty wave of intense difficulty wash over us.

Breathe and let it come.

The pain won't knock us over. It won't crush us.

No.

It will sand us down and shape us into ourselves.

It will polish us to shiny imperfection.

It will heal us.

Let it come.

Sit in the fires of your struggle.

Sit in the fires of your grief and desperation and loneliness and disappointment and heartbreak.

Let it burn you.

It's not so scary; it will only burn away what you don't need anymore.

Howl to the moon, shout to the breeze, unclench your fists, and let go.

Your Broken Heart is Art

Within the ashes of pain, there is beauty: your shining and unquestionable beauty.

There is treasure.

There is a rose that sings of inspiration, hope and joy.

There is love.

Don't ever think that a bad day or a tough week or terrible news or a shitty year means your life is fucked or that you're fucked.

Crappy moments and crushing discomfort are the most brilliant teachers.

Taste their wisdom and bow to their lessons.

Struggle comes and goes, just as happiness comes and goes.

Dance with what presents itself to you, it's your medicine.

And

Keep.

Going.

40.
This is for the Tough Days

This is for the days when our hearts hurt like hell, pulsating with a fierce, fiery pain.

This is for the days when we bite back tears, trying too hard to swallow them whole.

This is for the days when our souls feel heavy, so we slump our tired shoulders down, down, down.

This is for the days when getting out of bed feels like a bad-ass, award-winning achievement.

This is for the days when we tremble with anger, our temper on super-short hairline-triggers.

This is for the days when we feel empty, useless and invisible, like a hungry ghost.

Yes.

This is for those really tough days.

The days that rip us wide open, leaving us naked and exhausted, shivering in the dark.

The days where we just want to give up.

The days where we want to run far, far, away.

But, we can't.

We can't run. Or hide. Or give up.

Because if we did, the only person we would be running from is ourselves.

We would be giving up on ourselves.

Hiding from ourselves.

So, yes, we can try to bail and haphazardly fling ourselves under a fast-moving bus when the going gets tough.

But the thing is—we actually need ourselves the *most* on those fucking tough, trying and terrible days.

Let's stay.

Let's stick it out.

We don't need to understand what we're feeling.

We don't need to analyze it.

We just need to stay and support ourselves.

How?

What can we do?

We can be bold and dive right into the toughness of the day, feeling the icy water drip into our hearts, freezing to form incredibly beautiful icicles.

We can run directly towards ourselves, sprinting with wide open arms, a supportive smile and a glass of succulent red wine.

We can buy our battered souls a big bouquet of blossoming flowers.

We can clear a space and cry a thousand crystalline drops till the skies clear and our salty tear-rain has passed.

We can run our soul a frothy bubble bath, slip into mile-high lavender bubbles and take a breath.

We can retreat from the world, burrow under our covers, sigh, moan and just hurt.

We can ask ourselves, "What can I do for you right now?"

We can be really ballsy, wear our heart on our sleeve and ask a trusted friend for an extra-large serving of support.

We can curl up in child's pose and cry into our yoga mats.

We can write, paint, dance and sing our hurt, our passionate pain, our wicked grief, and express it no-holds-barred, creating magical art from our madness.

We can cue up an angsty, melancholy playlist and sob or scream or tremble till our hearts slip into a soothed state.

We can reach out, take our own hand and squeeze it hard.

Yes.

There are a thousand beautiful things we can do to support ourselves.

So let's vow now to never, ever abandon our sweet selves again.

Ever.

Because, yes, some days are incredibly tough.

But they can be really juicy, too.

They can be transformative.

They can be beautiful.

They can be filled with inspiration.

They can be chock-full of creativity.

They can be exactly what we need.

So, let's be bold and stick around.

Let's be badass and meet those tough days head on.

41.
Use the Blessing of Heartbreak to Create a Brilliantly Beautiful Life

He or she is not yours to keep.

They never were. They made sure of that.

Some paths cross and intertwine for what seems like a split-second—and we want it to last longer, we get down on our knees and pray to the wet, dewy earth because it seems like everything would be perfect if this love could just last forever.

The truth is, love dies. It withers. It evaporates. It rises into the sky like rainwater and becomes something new.

It's a cycle we hate.

Because it's nice and comforting to think that a relationship should go on forever, that it's infinite—but most of the time, love is a chapter, a single sentence, a page, a riveting, prose-soaked paragraph—not a whole book.

Most of the time, love is temporary.

What a goddamn tragedy, right? But it doesn't have to be. It can be beautiful. It can be inspiring.

Yet so often, we sit alone in our rooms, tears pouring from our eyes, trying to pull together the frayed edges of a broken love and weave it into something real, something that would make us less lonely, something that could mean something deeper.

We obsess over what could have been, what could have worked, if only this, if only that and *blah, blah, blah.* Maybe they *were* the one, after all?

Maybe. But mostly, that's bullshit.

There has to be a better way to live. And there is.

It starts with the truth: it didn't work out. If it would have worked, your hearts would be together right now. There would be no question. There would be no attempting to glue things back together with your tears and shaky hands.

When love is broken, *let it be broken.*

And yes, your heart might be broken, too. But it's okay. It's so okay, in ways you can't taste yet. It's a blessing. And I know it hurts, it hurts like hell—disappointment crashes around you like fragile china.

But it's okay. Set it all down. Set down the grief. The pain. The gut-wrenching agony of everything you've been carrying around.

Set it all down. Just for a second.

Breathe.

Feel tingly new life and promising possibilities pour into you with every inhale—feel stale air barrel out of you with each exhale.

When you're ready, release your hands from the clutching, the clinging, the clawing onto fumes of what could have been. Use the depths of your pain to weave something new—like maybe, your own dreams.

What is your deepest, most delicious passion?

What does your soul taste like?

What do you want to leave behind when you die?

Redirect your energy.

The energy of heartbreak is as intense as a crashing sea, and if harnessed properly—it can be a magical time of awakening. It's not about suppressing pain or pretending like we aren't hurting— but rather, to gently spin the rawness of that energy in a new direction—in the direction of growth, meaning and inspiration, rather than the exhaustion of lackluster longing.

We spend so much time worrying about love. *When it will come. When it will end. Why did it end? Do they love us back? Will he call? Will she reject me again?*

We need perspective. We need to zoom out. We need to do other shit. Awesome shit. Breathtaking shit. Soul-igniting, toe-curling shit that makes us smile a smile so big it could swallow the stars and crack open the sky.

I know we always say life is short, but it's long, too—strung together of hours and minutes and seconds that can feel very long indeed, like watching paint dry, when we feel uneasy in our bones.

So how do you want to spend your hours, your minutes—your life?

Open your eyes. There's a whole, vast, wonderful world out there to explore. To experience. To taste. To fall in love with.

There are evergreen mountaintops, joyous friends, wet forest floors, and the comforting sweetness of family. There are poems, melty mango sunrises and even meltier, mouthwatering sunsets. There are juicy hugs, inspiring ideas that change our lives, the earthy smell in the air after it rains, stranger's smiles, travel, disease, poverty, and death. I know, it's not all pretty.

But it's real. And our worries about love? Well, they're not always so real.

Stop, for one second, searching and longing so hard for love—stop obsessing, overthinking, and exhausting yourself in a sea of sputtering worries and fragile hopes and a thousand what-if scenarios.

Relax, sweet soul. Settle into your skin instead.

Settle into your delicious skin so deeply that you begin to hear the hushed whispers of your spirit spring to life.

What if you searched half as hard for your dreams as you do for love?

What if you searched for your soul instead?

What if you delved inside and found the gritty, wild passion that drives you?

It's all about energy. Where do you want to put yours?

Is there a gorgeous passion that sings to your soul?

Is there a way you could benefit the world, in some uniquely beautiful way?

Do it.

Now's the perfect time to do all the awesome things you always said you would, but never actually did.

Paint yourself to luscious life, in the most inspired way ever. Redirect your energy to your own heart. Reconnect with your wildest, most succulent dreams. Invest in your soul. Tend kindly to your needs as you would a sexy new love interest.

Use the blessing of your heartbreak to create a brilliantly beautiful life.

And the wildest, most infuriating thing of all is that when we are lit up — energized, galvanized and living our dreams with vividness — love will find us. It can't help but find us. It will smack us over the heads. Love will weave itself into everything we do, it will blossom all around us like lilacs in the Spring.

But take this time for you. *Just for you.*

Take this time — not just so you can one day find love — but so you

Your Broken Heart is Art

can find yourself.

It's all about energy.

Where do you want to put yours?

PART 4: SHE. IS. SOARING

42.
And Then She Left

Maybe she was better at leaving than staying.

Maybe she had made a huge mess of things again.

All she knew was that her lungs were so tired of breathing in the suffocating scent of stale air and sour memories—she needed fresh evergreen breezes and the wild expanse of new possibilities.

Was she a coward? Or, was she courageous?

She didn't give a damn either way.

She was ready to do what she needed to do for the sake of her soul.

She wasn't afraid to wipe the slate clean. She wasn't afraid to tell the past to go fuck itself. She wasn't afraid to go off solo and spread her wings in a brand new way. She wasn't afraid to follow the tenuous threads of her dreams and see where each glittering fiber would lead—whose paths she would cross, what explosions of love and gritty truth she could create.

When life becomes a suffocating prison, we always have the option to break free.

She knew this, in the feathery depths of her falcon soul, from the trembling heights of her wandering spirit, from the rocky valleys of her flowing tears.

She moved with the wind, with the melting shadow of the sun—
She moved when the whispers of her heart told her to.

This could seem like a lonely, nomadic existence, but it was not lonely for her.

In her mind, there was no richer company than the open road, the whipping winds dancing through her hair, the seductive song of the strawberry sunset in her rearview mirror and the restless chatter of dreams filling her ears like the excited buzz of poems not yet written.

She left.

She left everything behind. She crossed cities, small towns, and state lines.

She left behind frayed friendships and mistakes and loves gone terribly wrong,

She left it all behind in the blink of an eye.

She was not sad.

It would have been nice and pretty to say that she was devastated with grief, but she wasn't. Her tears were of blossoming hope; they were not tinged bitter with the sting of regret.

For her, goodbyes always held this wild sort of magic, this tingly influx of raw energy. She could sense the buzzing lilac scent of new possibilities through each sticky layer of pain and feel new life budding—ruby red, streaked with purple, sprouting lush emerald leaves, growing tenderly—in her veins. If endings were like the icy depths of winter, new beginnings were like spring.

And she was so ready for spring.

So she left.

She left in a lightning flash, in a mad dash of hope. She stormed outside like the fiercest wind, and moved the hell on.

She let the harsh pain of the past slip through her fingertips, like scratchy grains of sand. She had suffered long enough—for far too long—and she was done torturing herself, blaming herself mercilessly for everything. She was done apologizing for who she was and holding tightly to the tattered ropes of things that would never be.

She threw the ashen remains of the confused girl she used to be, of all the tough shit she had been through, to the fingernail edge of the crescent moon—a gesture of truth and forgiveness and transmuted beauty.

And then, on the coattails of her own excited exhale, she left.

She rejoined her jeweled soul in a majestic mountain land, soaked with sun, speckled with evergreens. She walked forward, with brave feet, feeling a thousand pounds lighter, with fresh skin and a ripe, open heart.

Maybe she was better at leaving than staying.

Maybe she had made a huge mess of things again.

All she knew was that her lungs were so damn tired of breathing in the stale scent of sour memories. She needed fresh evergreen breezes and the wild expanse of new possibilities.

And so it was.

She said goodbye to a life that was never hers.

She said hello to the sparkling emerald seas of destiny.

Because she had always known that when our days start to feel like a suffocating prison, we can break free.

So she did.

And freedom, oh sweet freedom—it tasted more delicious than she'd ever dreamed.

43.
Because Now She Remembers

You forgot, didn't you?
You're not just a mess.
You're not just a woman barely holding it together while muttering curses under your breath. You're not just heartbroken, sad, tired, or lost.
You're a force of nature
Gathering strength like a cyclone
Your hair in tangles
Emotions coming in gusts
Dragons panting from the fire of your breath
Falcons diving at a thousand miles an hour
When you shake your hips
As the past peels off
As you dive deeper, deeper
And face it all
The gritty pearls of this life—
The pain
The horror
The loves lost
The loves gone terribly wrong
The pain, yes
The pain you inflicted on your Self because you didn't remember.
Because you thought you were worthless
Because you didn't know you deserved plushness and nectar

Because you forgot.
But you remember now, and that changes everything.
The pain was just your initiation.
It was dipping your toes in the exquisite salt waters of your becoming.
There is a pulse, a song
You've been dancing to
Writing this whole time
And it's *not small.*
It's glittering, it's grandiose, it's soaked in truth and seeded in stars
Your rising is imminent
It is written in stone
Your rising was guaranteed by the fire you kept alive
Even when you didn't know that's what you were doing.
Because you remember now.
You remember dancing naked
You remember flying
You remember hearing the whispered secrets of trees
You remember taking the ache and making it into gold
You remember kissing plants and pressing herbs to your skin.
You remember the shiver of divine knowledge swirling in the palms of your hands like fragrant oils
Vow to the heartbeat of the earth, to the sublime green of the grass, to your Self
Not to forget anymore.
You're a witch
A wild woman
Maybe they've called you a bitch

Your Broken Heart is Art

Crazy for knowing that you know; for feeling what you feel.
You're a radical woman.
You're medicine.
You're so potent, honey, *and that was always true.*
You're a phoenix.
A destroyer, because you're a creator.
You're made of prayers and stitched of earthly power.
You give birth in the blink of your eyes when no one is looking.
You've kissed Kali and died to shed your skin a thousand times.
All you need to do
Is dip your head back
And let the nectar of the cosmos spill into you
As it's done a thousand times before
Your bones remember
Your blood remembers
What it is to taste of the earth and smell of the sky
What it is to slink your body like a snake
And divine the fate of nations with your dance
What it is to feel, to taste, to breathe, to be so acutely alive.
You are ancient
Wise, supple, and wild —
You are meant to flood the back of horses with your long hair and naked body
Galloping into the forest
As you listen carefully
To the hushed pulse of the river
The crescendos of the trees
The stillness of the meadows
The sweet songs of the fairies

You remember.
And you remember your sisters, as well.
Stand with them.
They surround you, in a circle
With candles and support as plush as velvet
And tears that shimmer under the light of the full moon
Because it feels so belligerently good
And you come home to the earth
To your luscious body
To each other
To the magic pressed inside you since forever.
Because you don't need to hide anymore.
Your magic is free,
You are free.
You stand tall now, aligned with your power, aligned with the earth.
And that changes everything.
Do you feel it?
This fresh, dewy emerging.
This boisterous birth.
The way we are waking up, together.
In yawns, whispers, moans and howls
So take your first free breath in centuries
It is safe
Take your first free step
You are beholden
Only the to the rhythm of the earth
And the wisdom that crashes inside.
Let no other lord over you.

"Because now she remembers," the sky pours out to you in poems lined with sapphire arms.
Let it be a declaration—
It echoes all over your skin.
It used to taste like pain
Now it tastes like the salt and blood of wisdom.
It tastes like rising.
It is the prayer that resounds on the lips of the earth—
"Because now she remembers."
Let it be a declaration
That shakes the trees
That vibrates through every blade of grass
And every pain
And every tear
And every hope
As it echoes and echoes
And makes the fragile places you inside weep with joy.
You are home.
"Because now she remembers."
Let it be the mantra of the Great Mother.
Let it be the fire
The truth
The love
That drips into the cracks and crevices of everything
At the tenderest
Light
Of
Dawn.

44.
For the Women Who Are Meant for More

Here's to the gritty, truth-seeking goddesses who aren't afraid to get their hands dirty.

Here's to the brave, badass ladies who have blasted through a nightmare of shit to be standing here today.

Here's to the earthy mamas who think stilettos are a sick fucking joke—

The luscious ladies who love feeling the raw earth beneath their bare feet, and bow down proudly to the supple, winding curves of their thick, fleshy hips.

Here's to the creative vixens who breathe their sun-soaked, moonlit, windswept, star-dusted dreams to life, *every damn day*— rain or shine.

Here's to the wise women who, time and time again, have chosen their own hearts.

I applaud you, with every fiber of my being. I honor you.

I am you.

We are strong and confusing, complicated and powerful, magical and maddening—we are meant for so much more.

We will never be happy stuffed in a sparkling white kitchen with

Your Broken Heart is Art

a floral apron, a sleek bun, and carefully applied pink liquid lipstick to complete the wax mask of our fake smiles, playing the role of perfect wife or perfect girlfriend or perfect mother.

Our hearts will choke. Our spirits will scream.

We will never be happy sitting in a grey office working 9 to 5, watching the clock tick slowly, while our souls shrivel to the buzzing sound of fluorescent lights, unable to breathe in the fresh, muddy scent of gusty winds and the frantic, jeweled sweetness of budding cherry blossoms.

We will never be okay sipping champagne, trying on haute couture, and talking about ways to make our asses skinny and recipes for dinner parties and how to get a man to love us.

We don't really give a damn about any of that—

We want to talk about soul. About dripping truth. About magic. About death. About struggle. About the world's heartbreaking pain.

We wanna stand in the billowing breeze and decipher wise whispers of the wind as it roars through each singing strand of our thirsty, messy hair.

Yes.

But, for a painfully long time, we have denied who we really are.

We have tried and tried and tried to squeeze our wild wings and paint-splattered hearts into the cramped plastic molds of what we "should" be.

How miraculously we have failed.

Why do we rip ourselves up into sad, feathery pieces, trying so hard to slide into pretty little lives that, quite frankly, don't even appeal to us?

Normal won't cut it—extraordinary is what we're here for.

We are meant to merge with the moon, cry with the rain, rise with the tides, and shine with every goddamn slice of shimmering yellow sun.

We are meant to run through crowded streets, with love in our hearts and tangerine scarves streaming through our fingertips as we dance to the sobbing drum of the world's crying tears.

We are meant to make art that grows gritty wings and inspires sad, closed hearts to break the fuck open.

We are meant to stick out our tongues in a fierce lion's breath in the most unexpected moments—

Rawwwr!

Our dreams and visions and destinies must come first.

Always.

Because we aren't here to play small; to be polite, people-pleasing pretty plastic barbie dolls with empty, lifeless hearts—we are here to make waves, to chase dreams, to stand in the blazing fires of truth—*and we know it.*

We are here to live from the harrowing depths of our souls.

Why deny it anymore?

Let's reach inside our supple skin and taste the thick river of bubbling magic that pulses through our veins like rubies.

Let's shed the suffocating lives that were never meant to be ours—the lives society has brainwashed us into tolerating, but are slowly killing our souls.

It's time to burn, baby, burn!

Let's make a pact with our hearts—a vow to listen to that inner spark of magic, of truth, of delicious fire that cannot be denied for a minute more.

Let us promise now—

To honor who we really are.

To be forces of femininity, of love, of sacred power.

To let our star-dust spirits rise—and soar and soar and soar!

Extraordinary flows through our veins. Normal won't cut it.

We are meant for so much more.

Badass, truth-lovin', dream-weaving sisters, let's stop smacking our spirits down and squeezing ourselves into suffocating roles that will never satisfy our thirsty, roaring souls—

We won't fit.

We aren't meant to.

Our wings won't slide through small doors. We are meant for so much more—

Our dreams and visions and destinies must come first.

Always.

Please, answer the rain-drenched, whispering wolf calls of your wild soul.

Do not let your wings lie sticky and suffocated, in a sad clump on the floor.

Do not let your vibrant spirit wither into a colorless grey existence.

Do not let your jeweled destiny lie dormant and dead.

Do not live the life you think you "should."

Fuck should—

Live the life that makes your heart beat louder, the life that sets your bones sweetly on fire, the life you can't stand not living—

Answer the blossoming calls of your wild soul!

Your Broken Heart is Art

Go, now—

Into the lush, emerald forest of who you really are.

Find yourself.

Discover your gifts.

Share your gritty magic with the world.

Follow the promising path of your courageous destiny.

Go—

Now.

Do not settle for an empty half-life.

Do not settle for good enough.

Do not settle for anything less than exquisite or extraordinary.

Oh, sweet wise, wild woman—do not settle—

At all.

45.
How to Touch Her

She is a thousand light pink chrysanthemum buds, poised to unfurl one by one, like an ancient scroll of poetry in your arms.

She is a valiant purple lotus, bursting through the mud in a symphony of sweetness and sheer will power.

She is soft, skin like silk—while her soul burns hot and raw, blazin' like a wildfire.

She looks at you with a gentle gaze and sees inside of you—the hurt, the strength, the pain, the tattered edges of chapters that you'd rather forget—and embraces *every single part of you* with love.

She isn't an angel, and she isn't your savior. But through the crowned glory of her deep femininity, she can—and will—change your life.

You have fallen under her spell—charmed by the way she is easily moved to tears, her vulnerability, the way she lives passionately, the warmth that envelops her when she is most herself.

How do you touch a woman like this?

A woman who knows she is magic.

Oh, how you long to feel her. To twirl her into your arms and press your body close to hers as the moon waxes full and plump, like the kisses and cabernet you'll share, staining your lips deep red, as your hearts swell with pleasure.

Maybe you want to pounce on her like a hungry tiger, *but waiting is better.*

How do you touch a woman like this?

A woman who makes you never want to utter any other lover's name again. Just hers. Only hers.

Go slowly. Touch her like you've never touched anyone before.

Touch her like it's the last thing you'll ever do.

Touch her like she is a storm about to sweep through the air, all promise, joy, and static electricity.

Touch her like she is a celebration of life itself—all confetti, rapture, and ripe, dangerous curves.

Touch her like you're weeping the tears you were always afraid to cry.

Remember, you are not getting—or taking—anything by being granted access to the luscious rolling landscapes of her body.

It is about sharing the experience.

It is about all the moments that lead up to kissing, caressing, and sex. The precious hours spent laughing. The adventures through mountain meadows. The stimulating conversations, leaving your souls perfectly exposed.

It is about trust.

It is about making her feel as safe as possible.

To touch a woman is to worship her. It is to pray, as you plant your fingertips upon her, at the altar of her fantastic soul.

So pray, with the frenzied joy of your entire being, your eyes locked firmly on her, your lips trailing a symphony of kisses all over her arms, thighs, stomach, and neck—kisses that take root deep inside of her, blooming into roses on the surface of her skin.

It is not about your selfish pleasure. Oh no, honey. It is about how every touch, every word, every whisper—can open her, petal by petal. It is about making springtime happen on her skin, her hips, inside her body, in her heart.

It is about respecting the vivid masterpiece she is.

It is about touching her dreams. Her regrets, mistakes, messiness, and sadness.

To touch a woman is to feel beyond her skin, goosebumps rising like magic from the gentle weight of your fingertips—as you breathe in the mysterious galaxy she is.

It is never about merely completing an act.

Oh, no...

It is about the joyous journey of connecting. It is about the utter sacredness of your limbs folded fantastically together, the feathery softness of her skin against the roughness of your beard—for your bodies are bridges to your souls.

It is knowing that when you touch a woman, when your fingertips trace the edges of her inner thighs—you are entering a sacred space.

Never forget this.

Every moment, every sensation is about creating more connection—and *this* is what makes it feel good.

Every touch has a soulful intention behind it—and this is what makes it feel really good.

Every kiss contains your entire, dripping heart in it—and this is what makes it feel really, really good.

Your vulnerability is the most important component. Your presence is required, one hundred percent.

And when you enter her—there is no rush. Feel everything.

Breathe together.

Feel inhales fueling her body, feel her essence dripping out. Feel what her body loves, what her heart needs. Follow her melodious moans like a map.

But know that *she* is the treasure. Not sex. Not finishing.

Simply being with her, knowing her, tasting her.

There is no manual. *She* is your manual.

After you make love—after your bodies lie spent and sweaty after joining in this epic dance of cosmic beauty—she should feel fantastic. And so should you.

Continue to connect. Hold her. Look at her. Don't get up right away. Don't fall asleep and face the wall in numbness. Lay together, limbs intertwined, hearts exposed. Trace her skin, connecting the dots of her scars and freckles, making constellations of all the atoms she is composed of—the hot passion and lilac softness and incomprehensible beauty.

To touch a woman is ecstasy. It is heaven. It is the most wonderful thing in the world.

Don't ever forget it.

46.
I Am a Woman. I Am the Medicine

I am a woman, she says.
The ancient sands themselves have written upon me
I am the mystery, she whispers.
I am the sorrow, the hope, the madness, and the joy.
I am the chaos, the complete and utter down-and-out despair.
I am the breakdown, the breakthrough, the anger, the agony,
and the warmth of a kiss shared between young lovers.
Nothing
Is too big
For the softness
Of my lap.

I am all of it, she says—
I am the dirt and the disaster and the prayers you thought were never heard.
I am the hot gusts of long-needed transformation.
I am the darkness.
The empty, lonely hollow bones that just want to just give up.
I am the profane, the irresistible, the seductive.
And I am all of the light, the magic, the laughter, the innocence, the purity.
I am
Both.

I am the flame
And the extinguishing.

I am the sparkle and the sweat.
The grit and the glitter.
Nothing is too big
For the softness of my lap.

For that is how much, how deeply, how broadly I love, she says.
I will love you when you are ravaged and writhing.
And I will love when you are rising
And plump with content.
It is all the same to me.
Because I see you
I have always seen you.

Because I am a woman, she says.
I am nature.
The destroyer, the creator, the mother.
I am a woman, she says.
I am not a feeble creature.
I am the funeral of your pain.
I am the strength you'll only ever find in the bleakest moments.
I am the love that pulls you through everything.
I am fucking unruly and surprising.
I am sweet.
Nothing
Is too big
For the softness
Of my lap.

No pain, no patriarchy, no sickness, no fear, no apathy, no disbelief

Your Broken Heart is Art

May it all rest on me,
For I will not hold it
It will dissolve
Through the fire of my frenzied breath
Like honey into holy water
And even the bitterness
Will be honored *so gently* that

It
Becomes
Sweet.

Because I am a woman, she says.
I wear dirt all over my body
And delight in it.
I am the stormy sky and the faintest streak of sun.
I am the tornado and the rainbow.
I am the wound and the healing scab.
The sting of betrayal and the first drops of forgiveness.
I am both, she says.
Do not cast me into any category.

Because I am a woman, she says.
I drip with magic
I shake with truth
And I seep with venom, too
Because sometimes
The poison that was placed inside us
Becomes not poison anymore
But power, beauty, love, and serenity.

I am woman, she says—
Nothing is too big
For the softness
Of my lap.

I am a woman, she says—
Do not turn away from me, for
I
Am
The
Medicine.

47.
She Came Back to life

"I love you," she said, as a blustery, cold breeze blew back her messy hair.

It hung around her shoulders in knots, strung together by sweat, by tears, by the sheen of mud on her face that spoke to the shit she'd been through.

But those words, those three powerful word—*I and love and you*...

First, she said them to—
Herself.
The darkness.
The time she spent underground.
All that she learned—who she was *not*.

The anger.
The pain.
The confusion.
The fear.

The tears, oh, the thousands of tears that had rained down her cheeks and made rivers.
The sorrow that twisted in her gut like nothing ever should.

And even there, in the muddy split, in the brokenness of it all—something had fluttered to life. Because even back then, when she felt that she was drowning, she knew it was more than that.

It was becoming—in the messiest, most primal way.

So she could love those tough times, she could love herself at the bottom of it all—but this did not magically make those times pretty.

It did not tie them up with a pretty, pink satin bow or make the pain okay.

Nothing will really make that okay—and yet, healing is still possible. That's the gift of it all.

So in those cool, jagged underground tunnels and spaces, she cried, she learned, she healed.
She fought for her life.
She fought for her voice.
For her spirit to rise up and blossom into the fiery breathlessness of spring.
She fought so hard for so long.

And one day, she realized she did not have to fight anymore.

She knew she could summon that blazing intensity whenever she needed it, sure—but she no longer needed to fight like hell to make it through the day.

Up, up, up
Out of the ground.

"I love you," she said
To that stunning, first breath of fresh air.

To that patch of golden sunlight on the just-sprouting blades of lime-green grass.

She stretched those weary muscles and put her feet on the warm, dewy grass, smiling faintly at the droplets of rain that hung heavy on the thin branches of the budding cherry trees. Sweet tears ensconced her. Finally, these were happy tears.

She came back to life.

Everything looked different. The world was no longer encased by a lens of anger or fear.

And it wasn't perfect, no.

But things looked vibrant. Enchanting. Safe enough.

So she took those tentative, excited first steps

And soon, the walking became dancing.

And soon, she realized how wise she had become

To drum on the beat of her heart

To listen to her body

To know what it is to squeeze the old crystals of pain and make them into beauty. Into art. Into passion and the stretching wings of ever-expanding growth.

48.
She Chose her Own Heart

She was angry for all the times he'd looked at her like she was too much.

All the subtle, whispered hints that she needed to calm down, tone it down, and be less real.

Maybe he'd never moved his lips and said it outright, *"Be smaller. Be quieter. Be less yourself."*

But he had said it with his eyes, his energy, his constant fear of the immensely powerful woman she was.

It hurt.

Secret fire rose up inside and blessed her with its wisdom. She began to think about all of this a little bit differently...

Because so what? Her soul spilled out into the streets, her heart was embroidered permanently in neon wildflowers on her sleeves.

So what? She wasn't a cute little kitten who could be watered-down into the precious image of what he wanted her to be. Yes, she loved incredibly fucking fiercely. She felt deeply and was achingly honest about the emotions that washed through her, like currents of salty ocean water daily.

Your Broken Heart is Art

So what?

None of that is heartbreaking at all—but what *is* heartbreaking is that she ever entertained the idea of changing for him.

That she thought it was okay to dull herself down for him.

What is really goddamn heartbreaking is that she denied her soul's truth, letting its decadent, divine juiciness wither up, for him.

Oh, the many misguided things she did to keep this relationship alive—as she herself, shriveled slowly.

Sleeping next to him every night, a million icy miles away; catering solely to his needs, forgetting entirely about her own.

It wasn't right, it didn't feel right.

But she tried so hard to make it right, to stitch right-ness into all the things that felt so terribly wrong.

She tried so hard to be good. To say all the things he wanted to hear—to be all the sweet, perfect things that would make him happy.

But she wasn't born to be good. She was born to be real.

She was born to be split-open, dangling on the crescent edge of life itself.

She was born to feel, to love, to break free, to bloom, to explode, to shine—to taste the sunset in her heart and feel the sea pulsate in her throat and roar her deepest truth through a thunderstorm of magnetic intensity.

She wasn't born to be good.

But she tried, for him–she tried too hard…

She tried until it broke her. She tried until she was pale, lifeless, and constantly tear-stained.

She tried until she became a small, repressed watercolor fragment of the neon masterpiece she truly was.

But one day, she stopped trying.

She looked in the mirror—her mouth gaping wide open in shock, for she could barely believe the lifeless ghost of a reflection that stared back at her.

What a goddamn wake-up call.

Her vibrancy was nowhere to be found. Her warm, electric smile was absent. The sparkle in her eyes was overgrown with black vines of grief.

She vowed to find it all again—to find herself again. Immediately.

She vowed to find joy, purpose, truth and meaning. She vowed to find the enchanted ember of spirit that still glimmered, thirstily, deep inside her.

So she stopped trying, and she started *being*.

Being raw. Being wild. Being open. Being herself.

And on this day, this love—if that's what you could even call it at this point—died. On this day, she became vibrantly alive.

She apologized exactly *not at all*—and walked meaningfully out the door. She strode fabulously into the arms of her soul.

Maybe she had waited her whole life for the stunning freedom of this moment.

For it was no longer acceptable to stomp out the flickering tangerine flames that yearned to encapsulate her.

It was no longer acceptable to forsake her insatiable appetite for life, for passion, for adventure, for the glorious gritty madness of truth—and constantly give away all of her precious time and energy to another, just to keep a half-hearted love affair alive.

It was no longer acceptable at all to live in a compact, grey shadow when she was destined to step into the pure lemony radiance of sunlight.

Maybe she had waited her whole life for the stunning freedom of this moment.

She stopped trying, and she started *being*.

And in the wide arms of this spaciousness, new choices revealed themselves.

She chose to be as exactly as loud and gentle and vivid as her soul told her to be.

She chose to only ever be with a lover who wanted *more and more* of her—not less.

In a tornado fury of soulful truth,

In a misty rainforest of pure poetry,

She chose herself.

It hurt, it ached, it felt foreign—the pain of letting go of what she thought she wanted, the pure terror of holding onto the deepest truth of what she really needed.

But it was far better than paying the bitter price of pleasing and appeasing a lover, just to have someone to keep her warm at night.

She could take the cold.

Hell, she welcomed the icy gusts of whipping wind, she would feel it with the entirety of her being—

Because it was real.

And after trying so hard for so long—she wanted real.

So she chose her own heart—the bruises, the shadows, the beauty, the pain and all.

She chose the gorgeous, multifaceted reality of her own heart.

It reverberated under her rib-cage, a ruby sea waiting to break free.

It spilled out fantastically into lush mountaintops and echoed into emerald valleys dotted with evergreens.

She chose her own heart.

It was the hardest and most beautiful thing she ever did.

Would she regret it?

Not for a single second.

.

49.
She Dives Deep to Be Reborn

She goes to the deep parts of the forest, the parts you fear, where the thickets are wild and prickly.

The parts of the forest that are uncharted, untouched, and untamed—where the truth lies wild and unvarnished, split-open and out in the open, like her feelings.

Oh, yes.

She goes to the place where she can feel the ancient fire inside her soul.

And that's when the drums start

And she dances

And cries

And finally lets herself feel it all.

She falls to the earth, she rises towards the sky.

She does not fear being too gritty

She does not fear coming undone

She does not fear how she looks

It does not matter *at all.*

For once, it is all about how it feels.

It is all about the pure and utter realness, the honest expression of it all.

It is about the joy, the sweaty pain, the laughter and anger

The truth, *her truth.*

'Cause the parts of her that other people have tried to take—well, they never succeeded—not really.

Not at all.

For she is intact—full as the ripe moon. She is glorious, this phoenix rising.

She is here.

She roars into the night—

And the mountains, the cool breeze, the damp, dewy grass, the mud and fresh, fragrant blooms in every color—they hear her.

She is heard.

The earth is here, in this darkest yet most precious hour.

The hour of her undoing, the hour where she yells

Fuck it

To the laundry list of other people's expectations.

Who she once tried to be

To please everyone else

Burns to the ground

And who she truly is

Emerges

Fresh, bare and soaked in the jeweled richness of moonlight.

It is incredible. Fierce. Dripping in dangerously deep aquamarine waters of authenticity.

Now, she can lay her head down onto the earth.

And fall asleep knowing how powerful she truly is—

As the heartbeat of the earth

Reaches up to meet her like ivy.

She is so held.

If there was one thing she would never forget—it is that she is held.

Through it all.

The earth welcomes her laughter, her howls, her pain, her rage, her whispers, and her tears.

It is not too much. She is not too much.

She is not too passionate, too emotional, too raw, too vulnerable, too weird, too sensitive, too anything.

In this most raw hour—she is completely herself.

All masks cease to exist

They go up in smoke

She unfolds naked, into the breathless wonder that was always written inside her soul, in permanent, midnight blue ink speckled with stars.

And goddamn, there was never anything more beautiful.

50.
She is Not

She is not here to make you smile.

She does not exist for the sole purpose of making your life easier or making your pain feel less painful.

She does not wake each day to make you gasp or groan with pleasure.

And she sure as hell is not destined to hold your broken pieces politely together.

She is here to inhale her pain and exhale

Fire.

She is not a pretty plaything

Or a sweet little pet

She is a living, breathing, booming woman

With curiosity flowing through her veins like hot pink lightning,

With thorns on her skin

And colliding particles of electric, mystical mystery in her eyes.

She might look cute, she might look delicate and sweet

But she's got a fierce beast inside her—

Her wild heart.

But that's no secret.

Because she knows what she's not—

And she is not here to people-please until she dies.

She is not here to say pretty, glittery things that make people happy, but have no truth, no meaty substance.

She is not here to hold the crushing weight of the world on her shoulders.

She is not here to hide the flames of her anger behind sweet, sugary, fake little smiles.

She is not the one who will save you.

She knows that she can't save anyone, for she nearly lost herself while trying to mend the rips of a thousand broken hearts.

Now, she knows—

She is here to love herself, first.

She is here to inhale pain

And exhale

Fire.

She is not a pretty plaything

Or a sweet little pet.

She is a living, breathing, booming woman

Sent here with a mission, a purpose, a spark

That blooms inside her

When she stops trying to be perfect

When she stops trying to say all the right things

When she stops trying to please everyone else—

When she stops, lets out a delicious roarin' scream and asks herself aloud—

What do I need?

A bright purple lily blooms in her chest,

It unfurls with decadence and sparkles proudly in the sun, it covers her skin with a silky coat of electric goosebumps.

And in that moment, all is revealed—a scroll of tattered truths that make her heart beat a little faster—

She is here to dive deep and she knows it.

She is here to be so honest that it hurts.

She is here to stand alone, completely alone, and taste dripping

Your Broken Heart is Art

raspberry glazed sunsets and kiss dark stormy skies with her head tilted back in pure, ecstatic pleasure.

She is here to create works of raw, wild blooming beauty from the gaping cracks and smashed shards in her heart.

She is here to unearth grains of gritty truth from the stinging scabs on her soul.

She is here to love fiercely and unabashedly—without timidity, without fear, without pretending, without second-guessing.

She is here to rise above her piles of shit and learn to fly.

She is here.

This moment is hers—hers to catch like a tangerine speckled butterfly in the palm of her hands—

This moment is hers

Hers to kiss, to touch, to embrace, to devour, to make passionate love to.

And in this moment,

She is so vividly alive.

She is here to inhale pain

And exhale

Fire.

51.
She Is Your Challenge—If You're up for It

Maybe it's the way she always looks like she has a secret on the tip of her tongue.

Maybe it's the way she holds back, just a tiny, little bit, biting her bottom lip, saying nothing, but expressing absolutely everything.

Maybe it's the way her hair is always slightly messy, windswept—flowing free like a frothy waterfall, deliciously undone.

What treasures lie beyond the tip of her tongue?

What rubies swim in the vast, deep, dark ocean inside her?

What lush beauty lies, dormant and eager, beneath the scarlet sheen of her soft lips?

That is something you'll spend the rest of your life uncovering.

She is your challenge.

She cannot be figured out, over a glass of white wine, on a first date, in an hour. She cannot be figured out through body language, through words, through laughter—she can't be figured out easily, at all.

She's multi-layered. Complicated as fuck.

She's a luscious, colorful garden with blushing roses, budding fruit trees, bluebirds and monarch butterflies—a mountaintop meadow exploding with the first signs of Spring.

She's a desert—hot and strong and unrelenting as hell.

She's a mossy forest, deep and mysterious and richly emerald green, like the glint of her eyes in the afternoon sunshine.

She's the breeze, ethereal, messy, lyrical—a soft whisper of vulnerability.

She's a fierce howling lioness; a hungry huntress; a vicious, determined wolverine.

She's powerful. She's outrageous. She's afraid. She's brave. She's gentle. She's as badass as they come.

Her eyes look like they hold the seas, tumultuous and powerful, crashing with constantly changing waves of aquamarine and grey and sapphire—somehow wild and serene at the same time.

And that's just the tip of the iceberg—for with every question she answers, more mysteries lie unsolved—hanging in the air like budding lilacs, infusing your mind with an ambrosia of wicked sweetness like you've never experienced in your life.

Her presence alone is an elixir. And she knows it.

So, no—she won't give her heart to just anyone. She won't dole out slices of her soul like it's cheap candy.

She knows better.

And no, she's not interested in being your well-behaved sweet little kitten of a sidekick. She's her own damn superhero. And, if that scares the crap out of you, then good.

She's your challenge.

Maybe it's in the stubborn way she won't ever be told who to be. Or what to do. The way she stands tall like a gritty lotus, proud in her earthy, sensual femininity—wholly unashamed of the curves on her hips, delighted in the way her flesh spills over slightly from the sides of her blue jeans.

Maybe it's the way her whole face lights up when she speaks the sacred vines of truth in her mind.

Yes, she's your challenge, there's no doubt about it.

But falling in love doesn't always come easy for her. Maybe other men haven't valued her—or maybe she didn't yet value herself. Maybe other lovers deeply disappointed her with empty promises that did not mean shit in the end.

She's looking for something real; something deep and magical and true.

She's not easy. It will take care and strength and bravery and precision to get to know this woman.

Are you patient?

Good.

She'll blossom in your presence, petal by precious petal, like a salmon-colored rose.

She's your challenge.

Beware her thorns, for she is certainly not all soft bunnies and whipped cream—she's got a grittiness to her that only the earth itself can explain.

Maybe it's all captured in the way she dances through the mud and shit and pain and difficulty like a Summer thunderstorm—welcoming every raw raindrop to land on her tongue as she shakes her hips to the primal beats of rumbling thunder and sobs salty tears with the slightest smile on her face.

Maybe it's the way she doesn't turn away from the shattering vulnerability of the present moment, but breathes deeply, looks it right in the face and tastes this moment with her entire heart.

She's strong because she's been broken open so many times. She's gentle because she knows pain so intimately. She's wise because she's fucked up a lot. And she wouldn't trade any of that for the world—because every mistake and heartbreak transformed her into the wild and wonderful woman she is today.

She's magical, she's maddening, she's the kind of woman who knows the full extent of her power,

The kind of woman who kisses the dewy earth with every step

she takes,

The kind of woman who cares deeply, feels profoundly, and loves madly,

The kind of woman who will passionately argue with you 'till the warm, apricot glow of sunrise,

She's the kind of woman who will shock you to the core with a single smile.

She will make you question everything; she will be the delicious tornado that blows your perfect little world to bits.

Knowing her is an adventure that you have to be ready for.

Loving her is like breathing for the first time.

Kissing her is alchemy. Her presence alone is an elixir; her heartbeat heals the world; her tears make flowers bloom.

She's a masterpiece and she knows it.

She won't be easy, that's for damn sure, but she is more than worth it.

She is your challenge.

Are you up for it?

You have no idea the kind of mystical, life-changing beauty you're in for.

52.
She Said Yes

There is more than merely existing, watching time tick by, seeing the seconds fade away as they funnel quickly through our fingertips.

There is more than just getting through the day.

There is *living*.

And in that moment, in her bedroom, alone, in the pitch black of a sad, bone-chillin' winter night, in the midst of a stinging, fracturing heartbreak, she said yes to life.

Real life.

Not a sparkly, confetti-laced strawberry dipped fairytale fantasy—

Real life, in all of its real, gritty glory.

She sat in silence, watching her chest rise and fall, savoring the thumping of her heartbeat, hearing the hushed secrets of the swaying pine trees. She closed her eyes and she said yes—

She said yes to loneliness.

She said yes to change—the change that swept through her bones like a fierce, howling wind and made her muscles quake with fear and excitement alike.

She said yes to standing up and facing that fear.

She said yes to driving off into the apricot-singed, brandy-soaked sunset—alone—with no one but the long, curvy highway as her companion.

She said yes to pain. To beauty. To being brave enough to break.

She said yes to the teardrops that fell like a light Summer rain.

She said yes to adventures, especially the ones that seemed too risky, too scary, too crazy—those were the adventures she *most* wanted to take.

She said yes to life—

Yes to the chaotic, caring whispers of her soul.

Yes to her heart.

She threw her arms

Up, up, up—

To the tie-dyed sapphire sky

Tasting stardust and pain

She fell in love with life,

All of it.

Not the flimsy, sequin-covered socially approved bullshit

Your Broken Heart is Art

swirling in her head—

Real life, in all of its real, gritty glory,

Messiness, discomfort, tenderness, and all.

And slowly, very slowly, her days opened up, her heart revealed itself like a tender lily, and with her head tilted back under the jeweled cobalt sky, she smiled a smile so big it could swallow the sun—

She became illuminated again.

Because the days were no longer colored with the single-minded quest to find a lover, to avoid her truth, to desperately fill up the empty void inside her.

She sat alone, in simple silence, more content than she had ever been—icy wind dancing through her hair, tiny snowflakes landing on her cheeks, listening to the sound of her own heartbeat.

She came home to herself with gentle grace and remembered what she had known for so long.

This moment was her lover

This second was her soul mate

This life was *hers*

And she began

By saying

Yes

To this breath.

53.
The Aquarius Woman

A lightning bolt strikes, the sky clears, and Miss. Aquarius skips out of the smoky aftermath, with flowers in her hair and turquoise mala beads strung around her wrists.

Her long skirt flows in the breeze, and she breathes in, ready to take flight.

The world feels wide open, juicy and full of possibilities, just the way she likes.

She strums a guitar and laughs out loud, leaping and twirling and turning down the street.

She appears completely carefree, but— she holds a dripping aquamarine destiny in those delicate arms.

She bears a never-ending jug of water, sprinkling her wistful wisdom and luscious love and gentle encouragement to any thirsty soul that passes by.

How can she move so lightly?

How can she care so deeply?

She's a walking contradiction.

She's a social butterfly and a lone-wolf.

She's a humanitarian and a rebel without a cause.

She lives in her head, but has a huge, dripping heart.

She's hot.

She's cold.

She's here.

She's there.

She's frenetic, fierce, stubborn as hell, strong and fucking unstoppable.

Yes, she's light and airy— effervescent like extra-bubbly champagne.

But she's electric.

She is *goddamn electric.*

She's a shock-wave, a lightning bolt, a twirling tornado, a powerful pulse of electromagnetic energy.

She is no joke.

She will change completely in a fraction of a second, growing strange sparkly wings, shedding her skin ferociously to take flight into a whirling gust of wind.

Dare anyone think they own her?

Dare anyone try to keep her?

She's.

Gone.

She will never stand for a caged life, even if fighting for freedom hurts like hell.

She's born for the breeze and she knows it.

She is goddamn electric.

She will go outside and dance wildly in the world's sobbing tears, the salty drops soaking her vintage floral dress through and through, as she closes her eyes and drinks it in like nourishing mango nectar.

She knows that pain and sadness and shock and failure are inherently creative forces, necessary as air, inspiring as art.

She's unafraid of solitude and embarks on solo adventures, spreading her wings wide, breathing in the sacred spaciousness of crisp mountain air and salty ocean sunrises.

She's a wise woman, a mysterious creature, an intriguing mirage, constantly on the move, always ever so slightly out of reach.

But—behind her cool confidence and wild-child exterior, she's secretly scared and vulnerable and guarded as fuck.

She's secretly a lonely lone-wolf, looking for someone to cherish her unconventional, free-spirited soul.

She will find a fellow adventurer one day and bare her heart; it will be beautiful, like a breezy mountain meadow drenched in sunbeams, bursting with heavenly honeysuckle blossoms and bright wildflowers.

She will love passionately and strangely and freely and unconditionally.

But, she will always—first and foremost—be her own woman.

She will not belong to anyone.

Because she is not meant to.

She belongs to the breeze, to the stormy night sky, to the frenetic pulsing heartbeat of the entire world.

She belongs to starry nebulas and strange circus songs and shocking moments of revelation.

She's born to fly where lightning strikes.

She is goddamn electric.

54.
There's Nothing Like the Magic of a Woman

A woman is not to be known in one sitting. She is meant to be explored over a lifetime. Opened gently, like a magnolia flower in late summer, as each emerging petal is savored like saffron.

Her fragrance is sealed by the winds of fate, and it speaks loudly, even in silence.

Just from the multitudinous depths of her presence alone, you can smell her soul, like the ocean, from miles away. It is a breeze that just takes you somewhere you didn't know you wanted—no—needed to go.

So before you ask that question...you know the one, destined to rub her the wrong way—

Why is she so damn complicated?

Don't.

Lay down your confusion and rise to the occasion in a new way. Surrender to your senses; try a tactic that doesn't involve your mind.

Make knowing her a voyage—an exploration of the vast terrains that lie within her.

See, she is the sky. She is an entire book that is infinite and sublime, never finished, always writing and rewriting itself.

She is the sunrise and the sunset; she is the echoing strand of hope that is apparent in the thickest darkness.

She is a supernova. An entire solar system.

And when you dive into the honeyed stars of her smile, don't think that she is all angelic sweetness.

Oh, no—
She is also a hurricane. A mistress of death.

Watch her howl and cry and devour her demons and rise above the ashes in fire and fury; in love and glory.

Witness it all.

You will begin to feel this unshakeable truth that we never really know someone completely, because change is happening, always. Life is freakin' dynamic. We can only ever hope to keep getting to know someone as they shift and evolve and grow.

It is electric. It is exciting. It is fantastically hard to wrap your head around.

So don't ever stop getting to know her.

Get to know her over and over again, every moment, every day. Get to know her with your words, your actions, your touch, your questions.

And it's this mysterious quality you didn't know you were thirsty for—because there's nothing like the sweet magic of a woman.

It's maddening and perfect. It's shocking. It's wild.

Just when you think she'll zig—
She

    Zags.

Just when you think she'll be gentle as morning dew, she's a fierce warrior with determination blazing in her eyes.

Just when you think she'll shut down in ice, she licks her lips, circles her hips, and looks at you like a luscious sex goddess.

Just when you think you know her, new depths are revealed.

Don't be confused or concerned.

Be grateful she feels safe to reveal the vast seas of her true nature to you.

Honey, she is setting herself free, and she wants to share it with *you*.

About the Author

Sarah Harvey loves living in the mysterious mountains of Asheville, North Carolina. Through her messy journey of healing from trauma, she has found immense freedom and comfort in creativity. She believes in resilience. She believes in tenderness. She believes that sometimes, our darkest days lead to the most unexpected, breathless joy. She is finishing her Masters in Counseling and plans to work with kids and families, taking a creative, inclusive, and gentle approach. In her spare time, she enjoys hiking through curvy mountain trails, curling up with her two quirky cats, and gardening.

Website: www.sarahlousiaharvey.com,
Facebook: www.facebook.com/sarahlouisaharvey
Instagram: @sarahlouisaharvey
Twitter: @sarahlouisa214

Printed in Great Britain
by Amazon